The Monument Builders

The Emergence of Man

The Monument Builders

by Robert Wernick
and the Editors
of Time-Life Books

TIME
LIFE
BOOKS

TIME-LIFE INTERNATIONAL
(Nederland) B.V.

The Author: ROBERT WERNICK, a former staff member of LIFE magazine, is now a freelance writer who lives part-time in Paris, where he has long been an interested viewer of Europe's megaliths. He is the author of two novels and many articles on subjects that range from art to psychology.

The Consultant: BERNARD WAILES, Associate Professor of Anthropology at the University of Pennsylvania and Associate Curator of the University Museum, is a scholar of prehistoric Europe, with particular interests in rural economy and tribal society. Since 1968 he has conducted the excavation of Dun Ailinne, a "royal site" of the Iron Age in County Kildare, Ireland. His writings include many excavation reports and articles on prehistoric ploughs.

The Cover: Gigantic standing stones cast early-morning shadows across Stonehenge as a master-builder directs the final stage of construction, the erection of the bluestones that will form the monument's inner horseshoe of pillars. On a photograph of Stonehenge an artist has re-created the scene as a workman, using a measuring rope and a staff three megalithic yards long (8.16 feet)—like those carried by the master—determines precisely how far from the centre of Stonehenge the next bluestone should stand. Two workers in the background have already begun to excavate a pit in the chalky soil to hold the base of another bluestone pillar.

TIME
LIFE
BOOKS

Contents

Introduction

The great stone structures described and pictured in this book constitute one of Western Europe's most fascinating legacies. It has long been known that these cryptic works are of ancient origin, but new dating techniques indicate that they may be the oldest man-made monuments in the world. Despite their antiquity, they survive in astonishing numbers. While many have been destroyed or damaged, many more remain, as much a part of the landscape of certain European countries and islands as the hills and fields and villages. Even people uninterested in the remote past, and ignorant of archaeology, have some familiarity with these monuments simply because they cannot be ignored.

Theoretically at least, the very conspicuousness of these monuments should have made their mysteries easier to plumb. Yet the opposite has been true. For hundreds of years they have attracted the covetous attentions of quarriers and tomb robbers. Many have been almost levelled by farmers. Of the monuments that escaped despoliation, few were overlooked by the antiquaries of the 18th and 19th centuries. Many well-intentioned people published the results of their diggings and duly deposited the material they recovered in museums. But their work almost always fell far short of the standards of care exercised by the archaeologists of this century. As a result, much valuable evidence—some of the most ephemeral but telling kind—has been lost even from those earlier recorded excavations. We can only speculate how much has been lost from diggings that were never recorded. Thus, paradoxically, we know considerably less about most of these monuments than we do of many less prominent, though often better preserved, sites.

In the main, however, our relative ignorance of the monuments stems from the fact that their builders belonged to a preliterate age. In the total absence of written records, the human motives and intentions behind their construction and use are extremely difficult to fathom. Imagine, for example, how hard it would be to understand the faith and tenets of Christianity solely from the structures of ruined churches, and from the excavation of cemeteries.

The beliefs and rituals of the builders of these Late Stone Age and Early Bronze Age monuments, then, must be inferred from the monuments themselves, and from their contents and decoration where these exist. We may also try to draw certain inferences from ethnographic analogy, historical allusion and folk culture. Obviously, this is no easy task, and for the most part the inferences must remain shadowy and open to argument.

In any event, the monuments are truly remarkable. Though we understand much less about them than we would wish, they are an undeniable part of the European heritage. If recent hypotheses concerning the geometric layout and astronomical purpose of some of the monuments are borne out, their builders will merit a place of honour early in the mainstream of Western scientific development. Beyond doubt, the monuments reveal architectural and engineering skills of a high order, particularly since most were built without the benefit of a metal technology. Each new careful excavation, revealing further details of these ingenious structures, adds to our respect and admiration for the men who fashioned them.

Bernard Wailes
University of Pennsylvania

Chapter One: A Mysterious Legacy in Stone

Spread in an enormous arc across the profile of Western Europe, nearly 50,000 curious constructions in stone command the landscape of a dozen countries, compelling attention by their mass, their strange abstract beauty and their diversity of form. Many seem, at first glance, to have been shaped by some accident of nature. But all were fashioned by prehistoric man, as purposefully as the cathedrals of a later era. Though in many cases, such as the tomb entrance at left, the stones have yielded up the secrets of their purpose to the diggings and deductions of scholars, they still retain their air of mystery. Each slab, each oddly shaped boulder hold irresistible intrigue, raising a hundred questions and giving forth only a few grudging clues. And of all these ancient structures, the most complex—and the most tantalizing—is Stonehenge. The great grey jumble of stones, hulking out of the mist in the rolling grasslands of southern England, lie piled like a giant's building blocks. Their patterns of uneven circles and broken horseshoes are "so confused", wrote the Elizabethan poet Sir Philip Sidney, "That neither any eye/Can count them, nor any reason try/What force them brought to so unlikely ground."

For thousands of years the stones have posed their monumental riddle to all who passed by. The Anglo-Saxons who fought King Arthur and the last of the Romanized Britons paused on Salisbury Plain in Wessex to look with awe at this "unlikely ground". They

A durable reminder of the skills of the monument builders, this chiselled stone ring in Cornwall, England, may have served 3,000 years ago as the entrance to a burial mound. The hole, only 24 inches wide, was perhaps kept narrow in the belief that it would prevent the escape of dead spirits. The slab beyond probably helped support a now-vanished roof.

gave it the name Stonehenge—the "hanging stones"—because the huge crosspieces poised on massive uprights seemed to be suspended in mid-air.

One of the earliest attempts to explain what those hanging stones were doing there occurs in the *Histories of the Kings of Britain*. Geoffrey of Monmouth, a garrulous 12th Century writer who loosed the stories of Arthur and his exploits on the consciousness of Europe, had access to stores of traditional Celtic lore. In that lore he found a tale of how the stones were brought from Ireland by the arts of Merlin the Magician. They were intended, the legend said, to provide a suitable memorial for British warriors who had fallen in battle against the Saxon invaders.

In the eight centuries since Geoffrey, scholars and poets, historians, visionaries and simple sightseers have fashioned any number of new theories—plausible, fanciful or simply absurd—to solve the mystery that confronts every visitor to Stonehenge. What people in the unrecorded past could have been capable of construction on this scale, in this style, at such a place? Stonehenge has been attributed not only to Merlin but to Druids, Romans, Danes, Phoenicians, Egyptians; to giants and fairies and refugees from Atlantis. It has even been credited to crews of flying saucers from outer space.

Explanations of the purpose of Stonehenge vary just as wildly. The place has been interpreted as a temple to the sun, to the moon, to a snake god. It has been called a palace, an observatory, an assembly hall, a cemetery, a switchbox for the earth's magnetic currents, a cattle pen, a computer, a dance floor, a sacrificial altar, a marketplace and, perhaps most heroically, the poles for the tent of Caesar.

Stonehenge of course could not have been all these

things, though it may well have been more than one of them. Archaeological research has at last begun to clear the picture a little, to bring it from "utter Darkness to a thin Mist", as the antiquarian John Aubrey described his goal three centuries ago when he made the first accurate survey of Stonehenge. Why Stonehenge was built is still disputed. But archaeologists now know (or think they know) when it was built and by whom. And the facts turn out to be nearly as intriguing as all the fancies.

Nor does Stonehenge stand alone. It is only one of the most heralded of thousands of stone structures or monuments that once dotted Western Europe from Scandinavia to the coast of Italy, some of which were built as early as the Fifth Millennium B.C. Not all these are as mysterious as Stonehenge. In fact, the great majority are known to have been tombs used for interment of the dead. For more than 3,000 years —into the Bronze Age—the building of these great stone monuments went on. Then, gradually, at different times in different places, and for reasons not fully understood, the building stopped.

Until the 1960s most experts believed that these Western works were no more than crude imitations of monuments built in the East, in the Aegean and in Egypt and in Mesopotamia, the so-called cradles of civilization. But now a refined method of dating ancient objects has established that many of the Western monuments were built before the Eastern examples from which they presumably were derived. In a sense, this discovery requires that history be rewritten to include a new admiration and respect for the monument builders of early Europe—evidently they were a far more sophisticated people than anyone had dreamed. Not only did they execute marvels

of construction that have lasted to our day but the idea was theirs as well.

Such work took resources of planning and social organization of a remarkable degree. Not only were they imaginative and impressive builders, but the evidence at some sites—Stonehenge prime among them —indicates that the people also were dedicated students of the heavens. Their apparent grasp of astronomy surprises many scholars still; it seems to precede by centuries the development of such knowledge in the more conventional centres of civilization.

The task the builders set for themselves was monumental. Presumably they were not very much more advanced technologically than the present-day inhabitants of highland New Guinea. The earliest of them had no metal tools, no wheeled vehicles, no writing. Physically they were a small people, more wiry than robust. The earliest of them, in France and the British Isles, probably looked much as some Europeans of the western Mediterranean region look today—dark rather than fair, with sunburned faces and perhaps high-bridged Roman noses. (They had the tools with which to shave and trim their hair, but it is not known whether they did.)

They were hunters still—and burgeoning farmers. They lived off wild game, domesticated cattle, swine and sheep, which they herded through the unmapped wilderness, and grain, which they planted in their meadows and forest clearings. They had no machinery of state as we know it, though they must have had some system of authority, very likely consisting at first of rudimentary chiefdoms, in order to inaugurate such ambitious building schemes, assemble the labour required and carry out the projects.

Using stone hammers, picks made from deer antlers, shovels made from the shoulder blades of oxen, and perhaps fire and wooden wedges to crack the stubborn rock, they pried up boulders of immense size. Some were more than twenty feet long and one —the Grand Menhir Brisé at Locmariaquer in Brittany—weighed 385 tons. (Like many surviving monuments, that great stone is broken now into four pieces; perhaps it was struck by lightning or perhaps, being top heavy, it tumbled over as the builders laboriously heaved it into place.)

The builders left some of these boulders in their original shapes; some they hacked into rough cubes; some they decorated with strange designs that baffle the experts. They moved the stones great distances, using no motive force but human muscle, perhaps aided by domesticated oxen. At times they slid the stones downhill, or pushed them on wooden sledges over rollers made of tree trunks. Finally, at the designated site, they carefully levered the great stones upright, wedging the bases into prepared sockets dug into the earth, or hoisted them on top of other stones to form massive doorways and chambers.

A giant boulder used for construction purposes is called a megalith (from the Greek *megas*, great, and *lithos*, stone). Such boulders have been used all over the world for many millennia, whenever builders found them ready at hand. Many an ancient wall or modern pigpen can technically be described as having megalithic elements. But it was the Late Stone Age inhabitants of ancient Europe who made the first, the most ubiquitous and the most impressive use of such boulders. Though not every group of farmers and herdsmen in Western Europe built monuments, it seems fitting to speak of theirs as the megalithic culture. And this was a significant time in human history, for it introduced the concept of structures consciously designed to last forever.

In the days of their glory, when they crowned hilltops and forest clearings over thousands of miles of territory, the megaliths gleaming in the sun must have been a splendid sight. Very often they were built in the most conspicuous places, and sometimes it seems that deliberately conspicuous materials were used: blue dolerite, white quartz and golden-brown limestone. All the works were meant to call attention to themselves, to impress contemporaries and future generations alike. Very likely they were also meant to impress the immortal forces of heaven.

These proud structures go so far back in time that no memory of their original names survives. Today they are identified by a variety of titles that the local countrypeople have picked up from garbled historical recollections, legends and old wives' tales—such names as these: Wayland's Smithy (Wieland was the Germanic god of iron forging, and the megalithic tomb near Ashbury in England evidently reminded the Saxon settlers of a god-sized forge); Fairies' Rock; Dermot and Grainnè's Bed; Long Meg and Her Daughters; the Merry Maidens; the Devil's Arrows.

The monuments display a wide variety of forms and functions: from single stones to complex groups of halls or chambers; from tombs built for a single person to vast enclosures like the one at Avebury, north of Stonehenge, which one 19th Century scholar calculated could have seated an audience of 250,000. They can be divided into three very general categories as follows:

1. Monuments made of single upright stones, or menhirs (a Celtic word meaning long stone).

Menhir, England

Two dolmens in County Donegal, Ireland

Menhir, Dolmen and Circle

Though they vary greatly in size and shape, the thousands of megaliths in Western Europe fall into three broad categories. The simplest type is the menhir, a single free-standing slab of stone that may weigh hundreds of tons and range from two to 70 feet in height. The 10-foot, 9-inch specimen depicted here stands in Cornwall, England. It is now called the Blind Fiddler, a name inspired by a legendary musician who was turned into stone for playing on the Sabbath.

Menhirs that are grouped together, whether in a circle, a half circle or in rows called alignments, represent the second category of megalithic monuments. The stone circle pictured here, though smaller than the best-known example, Stonehenge, consists of 40 menhirs arranged in an ellipse that measures 107 feet in diameter.

The third type of prehistoric monument is the dolmen, a roofed structure. One of the forms it takes appears at top right in two graves built near Sancreed, Ireland. The larger grave in the foreground has three six-foot-tall slabs for walls, on which is balanced an enormous capstone that measures more than 20 feet across.

Stone circle at Castle Rigg, England

2. Groups of menhirs, sometimes in circles or semi-circles, and sometimes in parade-like ranks that stretch for miles. (Stone or timber circles surrounded by circular ditches and banks—a type found only in Britain—are known as henges.)

3. Finally, roofed structures, or dolmens (table stones). Dolmen is a rather loose word that sometimes—particularly in France—is applied to all megaliths without exception, a semantic confusion that has prompted at least one exasperated archaeologist to suggest that the word itself should be tied to a large stone and dropped into the sea.

Many of the roofed structures—the dolmens—contain bones and scattered tools, bowls and ornaments that appear to be offerings to the dead. So it has generally been deduced that most, and perhaps all, of them were tombs, though they may have had other uses as well. They vary in style among themselves as much as the tombs in a modern cemetery do, but their ground plans fall into three basic patterns.

The simplest, though not necessarily the earliest, is the single chamber. It is essentially a small room, round, rectangular or polygonal, roofed with flat stones or corbelling; in the latter roof pattern each stone partly overlaps the one below it until they gradually meet or leave a small hole at the top, often covered by a capstone. From within, chambers roofed this way look almost as if they were vaulted.

A second kind of dolmen is the passage grave. It begins with a corridor that may be as much as 60 feet long and is generally too low to allow a man to walk upright. This passage opens into a chamber that is usually wider and higher than the corridor; sometimes smaller rooms open off the main chamber. The chambers are often roofed with corbelling.

The third general pattern is the gallery grave, or long tomb. It has no entrance corridor; instead, the funerary chamber forms the whole structure. It may be wedge shaped or, more likely, a simple box, open at one end and quite a bit longer than it is wide. It may have a more elaborate layout, either curved or with transepts extending laterally from the main chamber, like chapels branching off the nave of a Gothic church. Some gallery graves have interior partitions that reach all the way up or halfway up to the ceiling of the chamber, and some sport circular openings cut in the stone of these interior walls.

Many surviving megalithic tombs are covered by mounds of earth; these are called barrows. Those covered by small stones are known as cairns. Sometimes these mounds spread and rise to the dimensions of a miniature mountain. Scholars believe that the great majority of the tombs were covered at the time they were built, and thus became rock-lined caves enclosed in artificial hills. But over the centuries the covering often has been reduced by natural erosion or by farmers and builders looking for soil and gravel. There are also some surviving tombs that bear no trace of any covering whatsoever. Have the dirt and stones worn away or been carted off? Perhaps not. They look so assertive in their nakedness that many authorities have suggested they were never meant to be covered at all.

While many contain skeletal remains, there are some—La Roche aux Fées (Fairies' Rock) in Brittany, for example—where no bones have been found. The acidity of the Breton soil may have corroded them, or early excavators may have removed them.

However they varied in shape, these monuments were clearly an important, even a vital, feature of

Three Basic Types of Tombs

Wherever the megalith builders flourished, there are tombs, some still covered by man-made mounds of earth, others exposed to the elements. However they may vary in details, they are generally of three basic types. A schematized example of each kind appears below in paired drawings that show the tombs in profile and from above.

The Single-Chamber Tomb

This simple structure has four stones for walls and one slab for a roof. Other single-chamber tombs may be circular or many-sided, but all have small interiors, seldom seven feet across.

The Gallery Grave

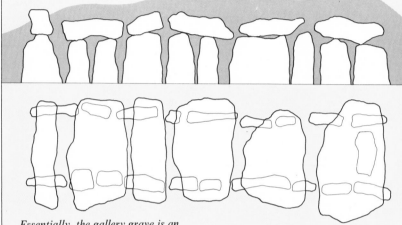

Essentially, the gallery grave is an elongated version of the single-chamber tomb. Burials were made along the tomb's walls, which may run parallel, as here, or narrow to a V.

The Passage Grave

Combining the other two types of tombs, the passage grave has a burial chamber, usually round, and a long corridor leading to it. In many such tombs the walls of the chamber section were built of overlapping stones, tapering to form a domed ceiling. The chamber resembles some dwellings and may represent an attempt to provide the dead with a permanent home.

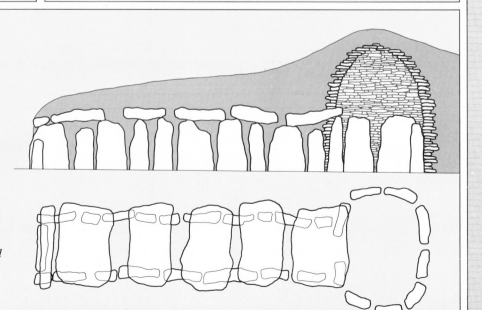

the life of the people who lived throughout Western Europe in the millennia before the dawn of history. Once they have been seen and studied, it is possible to sense some kind of universal idea—some cultural unity—that motivated their builders.

The monuments are rarely more than a few hundred miles from the sea, and are found in such disparate places as southern Sweden, Spain, Portugal, Malta and Italy. France has the greatest number, 6,000 in all, and Ireland and Great Britain have the richest variety. Of them all, the most frequently investigated —and perhaps the least understood—is Stonehenge.

It is today a gigantic wreck. Many of its original stones lie fallen, half-buried in the earth. Some have been reduced to mere stumps; others presumably have disappeared entirely. Stonehenge's construction, from the time of digging the first chalk embankment that surrounds it to the placing of the last towering columns at the centre, is believed to have lasted more than a thousand years—from 2775 to 1500 B.C. There is evidence of at least two large-scale rebuildings and many minor ones, as the architects and their hordes of workmen set up, took down and rearranged the pillars and lintels of blue-tinted volcanic dolerite and of hard sarsen sandstone from the neighbouring downs. "Sarsen" may originally have been a dialect use of Saracen, meaning foreigner or stranger. Or it may have derived from two Anglo-Saxon words meaning troublesome stone. Sarsens are found scattered over much of the chalk downlands of southern England, but no closer than 16 miles from Stonehenge. Actually they are the remains of a sandstone that once covered the area. When it was undercut by the erosion of an under-layer of soft limestone, it broke up into massive and jagged fragments.

Stonehenge is itself only the centre of a varied complex of ancient English ruins. Some, like the Cursus a half mile to the north, may be older. Shaped like a straight racecourse 100 yards wide and almost two miles long, the Cursus may once have been a processional path, perhaps for funerals. Other sites clustered near Stonehenge date only to the last days of the megaliths, around 1500 B.C. Among these are round earth mounds or funeral barrows—not megaliths themselves—which covered the luxurious burying places of Bronze Age chieftains. In the 1920s, aerial photographs of an area two miles from Stonehenge revealed a strange pattern in the soil: a group of six concentric circles. On excavation these turned out to be post holes for what must once have been an impressive wooden structure; indeed some of the holes still had bits of rotted stump at their bottoms. The best guess is that this circular structure may have been a roofed building, with a central court that was open to the sky. It could have been a shrine, or a marketplace or a council chamber—or all three. Naturally, its 20th Century discoverers named the site Woodhenge. In the 1960s, excavators came across the remains of at least three other structures of the Woodhenge type inside a huge earthwork henge only 80 yards away from the earlier find.

Seventeen miles north of Stonehenge is a ruin in some ways even more impressive. It sprawls over a much larger area and its surviving undecorated stones have a more primal, savage look than the carefully shaped stones of Stonehenge. It lies hard by (and encloses part of) the picturesque little village of Avebury. Over the years it has suffered more dam-

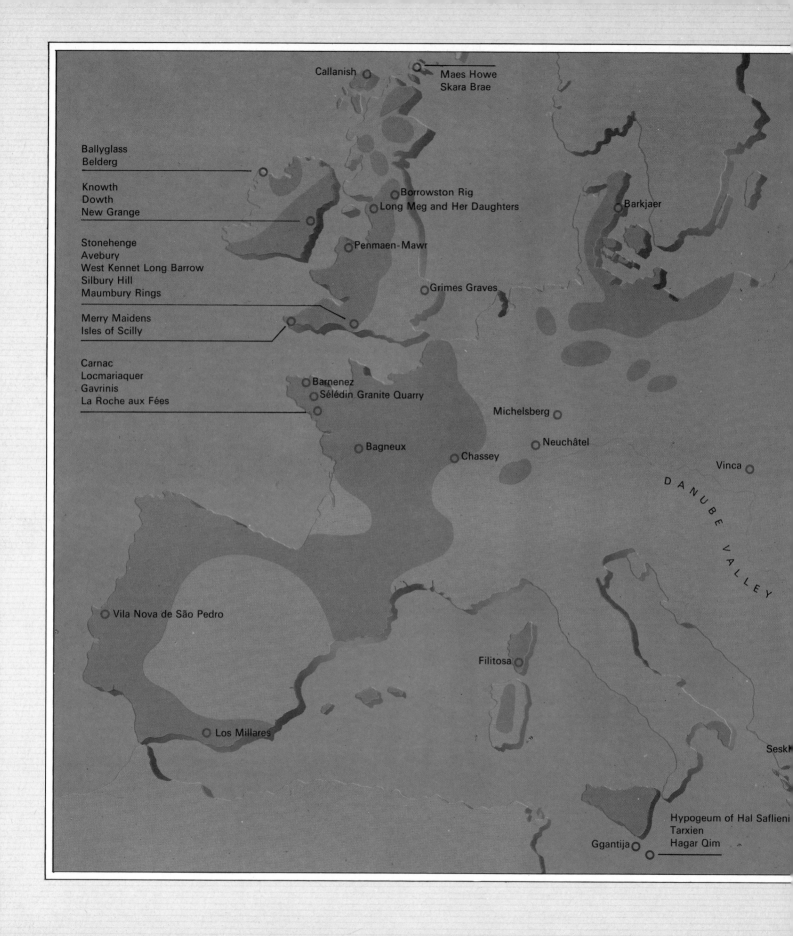

Callanish   Maes Howe
            Skara Brae

Ballyglass
Belderg

Knowth
Dowth
New Grange

Stonehenge
Avebury
West Kennet Long Barrow
Silbury Hill
Maumbury Rings

Merry Maidens
Isles of Scilly

Carnac
Locmariaquer
Gavrinis
La Roche aux Fées

Borrowston Rig
Long Meg and Her Daughters

Barkjaer

Penmaen-Mawr

Grimes Graves

Barnenez
Sélédin Granite Quarry

Michelsberg

Bagneux

Chassey

Neuchâtel

Vinca

DANUBE VALLEY

Vila Nova de São Pedro

Filitosa

Los Millares

Sesk

Hypogeum of Hal Saflieni
Tarxien
Hagar Qim

Ggantija

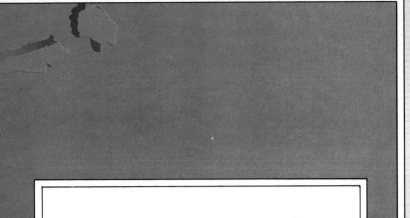

Mapping the Megaliths

Shaded areas on a map of prehistoric Europe emphasize graphically how megalith building spread throughout the area. Nearly all of the sites indicated here, from Maes Howe in the Orkney Islands off northern Scotland to Hagar Qim on Malta in the Mediterranean, are mentioned or described in this book. The monuments include a tremendous diversity of types—from simple mound-covered chamber tombs, to mighty circles or alignments of standing stones to the massive walls of fortified towns. In time they range over some 3,000 years, from some of the earliest-known passage graves at Barnenez in Brittany, dating to around 4500 B.C., to the Bronze Age passage graves of about 1500 B.C. on Britain's Isles of Scilly. Other sites lying outside the orange area were occupied by people who lived a similar way of life but did not build megaliths. Vinca, in Hungary, for example, was a major site of Danubian culture, and Sesklo, in Greece, is one of the earliest-known neolithic sites in Europe.

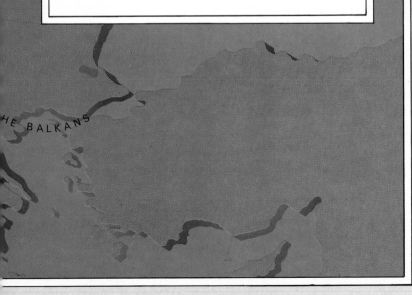

HE BALKANS

age than Stonehenge. Many of its stones have been dragged off to build houses or gateways. Originally there were three, and possibly four, stone circles at Avebury, but the inner ones have been almost wholly destroyed. The outer circle is surrounded by a bank and ditch enclosing twenty-eight and a half acres in all. It once consisted of some 100 sarsens weighing as much as 60 tons apiece. Unlike the sarsens at Stonehenge, these were never carved or shaped. It is obvious, however, that they were chosen with an eye for dramatic effect. Looming grey and misshapen out of the fog, or casting thick black shadows by moonlight, they dominate the countryside with their fierce, forbidding presence.

From the great circle at Avebury extends a double row of stones called the Avenue. It marches across a mile and a half of country towards a site called the Sanctuary. The Avenue is composed of tall, pillarlike stones on one side facing squat, diamond-shaped stones on the other, like so many male and female symbols. Of the Sanctuary, nothing now remains but traces of the holes dug for circles of wooden and stone columns that were successively erected there. Less than a mile away is West Kennet Long Barrow, a huge mound containing one of the largest of gallery graves. It is a five-chambered tomb with an impressive stone façade. At least 46 people were buried there before the entire structure was filled to the ceiling with chalk and rubble and five enormous slabs set up to block the entrance, as if to write finis to a chapter of human experience.

A half mile from West Kennet Long Barrow is Silbury Hill, the largest prehistoric artificial mound in Europe. It is 550 feet wide at the base, and its 12.5 million cubic feet of clay, turf and chalk rise 130 feet in a flat-topped cone, 100 feet across at the top. Archaeological probes into the mound have yielded no central burial, and the purpose of the monument remains a mystery. Yet the probes have revealed quite a bit about the sophisticated construction skills of the builders. Over a central mound of clay and flint covered by cut sod (which preserved enough vegetable material and insects to show that this phase of construction was done in late summer), they piled layer upon layer of chalk rubble. At each level the rubble was held in place by radial and concentric retaining walls of chalk blocks. Thus, despite over 4,000 years of natural erosion and the armies of sightseers who swarm over its surface each year, Silbury Hill has kept its original shape remarkably intact.

Roughly contemporary with the Stonehenge and Avebury complex in England are the passage graves of the river Boyne in Ireland. Housed in great mounds, they are a favourite subject of Irish mythology. In one tale they become the home of the high god Dagda Mór; in another they are the underground fortress-abode of "three times fifty sons of kings".

The three largest such mounds are at Knowth, Dowth and New Grange, and the latter needs no help from mythology to be recognized as one of the architectural splendours of ancient Europe. It sits in majesty on high ground above a bend of the river, a 36-foot-high cairn of water-rolled pebbles ingeniously stabilized by interior layers of turf—so much turf, in fact, that its builders must have stripped the topsoil off large stretches of farmland that they had tediously reclaimed from the forest. The mound is surrounded by the remains of a stone circle whose 340-foot diameter is identical to that of the smaller circles at Avebury. At the base of the cairn a set of 97 slabs, from five to 14 feet long, forms a continuous curb. On one flank an elaborately decorated stone, now pushed aside, once was used to close the entrance to the grave. From this entrance a passage runs for 62 feet, partway through the mound. The passage is formed of 43 stone uprights supporting 17 roof slabs that rise slowly in height as they approach the chamber. The corbelled chamber roof is one of the masterpieces of megalithic construction. At the narrow top, 20 feet above the much wider floor, the roof is sealed by a single capstone.

Chipped into the stones of roof, passage and chamber, and in the walls of three small chapel-like spaces opening off the chamber, is a riot of abstract designs: spirals, whorls, scallops, circles and chevrons. There are also stylized serpents and a set of strange rectangular shapes that have been variously interpreted as Phoenician numerals, old Irish inscriptions, masons' tally marks and a Scandinavian ship.

For a few days each year at New Grange, near the winter solstice when the days are shortest, the rising sun sends its rays through a rectangular opening above the entrance stone and down the full length of the long narrow passage. For several minutes the dark, undeciphered messages, even those at the far end of the chamber, are lit up, and the corbelled ceiling glows with an unearthly light.

Perhaps the sun was intended to light those designs only for the benefit of the respected dead who were interred there. But perhaps the living also were privileged to enter the chamber to partake of a divine visit at this time of the year. Indeed the symbols may represent the creed of a sun-oriented religious cult of which every other trace has disappeared.

Nearly 1,000 stones set in long rows mark the ruins of the Kermario alignment near Carnac. With almost four miles of such alignments, this section of Brittany has one of Europe's largest concentrations of megaliths.

Symbols much like those at New Grange were found carved into a passage grave on the island of Gavrinis, off the south coast of Brittany. The passage walls at Gavrinis seethe with spirals, ellipses and other curious geometric patterns. They have been interpreted as representing wombs or ears of grain or the very vault of heaven.

Gavrinis is part of a great complex of megalithic monuments found around the Gulf of Morbihan (Little Sea). The Gulf was formed by the settling of the land and the inrushing of the North Atlantic sometime between neolithic times and our own. Off the coast are megaliths whose tips can be made out at low tide. Perhaps these "drowned" stones are the origin of the Breton legend that says a sunken city lies offshore, and its cathedral bells can still be heard tolling undersea on stormy days.

North and east of the Gulf resort of Carnac is a region full of princely burial mounds and great stone alignments. Almost three thousand menhirs of all shapes—flat-topped, round-topped, pointed—snake over the moors in rough formations, 10, 11 and 13 abreast, usually ending in a semicircle or ellipsoid. At the eastern end of each formation the stones are no larger than sheep; they grow gradually in size until at the west they stand twice the height of a man. As always, local folklore has an explanation for these megaliths too. They are, the story goes, the soldiers of a Roman legion that pursued Saint Cornély, an early Christian, during an imperial persecution. When Saint Cornély's retreat was cut off by the sea, he turned and blessed his enemies. The gesture turned them all to stone.

Brittany abounds with similar stone alignments. Within a score of miles of Carnac are groupings of hundreds, and sometimes thousands, of stones. Apparently something about the regular files appealed to the people of Brittany the way circular forms appealed to the builders of England.

The early Bretons did not restrict themselves to rows, however. Within a short radius of Carnac can be found a profusion of megalithic treasures: the largest stone ever set upright, the Grand Menhir Brisé at Locmariaquer (now toppled); the tallest stone still standing, 39 feet high, at Kerloas; and one of the most luxuriant of all megalithic decorations, the interlocking spirals on the 13-by-20-foot capstone of the Table des Marchands at Locmariaquer.

To match the profusion and variety of stones in Brittany, one must travel south, around the farthest reaches of the arc of megalithic culture, to the Maltese Islands. The colossal structures crammed into two of these three tiny, rockbound isles, more fitted for goats than for human survival, are among the oldest, most complex and puzzling of all megalithic buildings. Like Stonehenge, they have no close parallels anywhere but appear to have sprung fully-formed from the native soil. Many must have been temples, though they all may have been tombs originally. In the Hypogeum (subterranean building) of Hal Saflieni on the island of Malta itself, remains found heaped in chambers cut into limestone indicate that 7,000 persons were buried there. As century followed upon century, these chambers were enlarged, new passageways were dug leading to new recesses and descending to new levels, until the finished structure was a three-storey, 33-room labyrinth. Within it are doorways carved in the shape of trilithons (crosspieces over two uprights, as at Stone-

Text continued on page 25

Mediterranean Monuments

Some of the oldest—and most ambitious—of megalithic monuments survive on the islands of Malta. The builders began as early as the Fifth Millennium with small, simple megaliths. By the Third Millennium they had completed some 30 monuments, many on a grandiose scale.

The floor plans of four impressive projects are shown here and on the next pages, each with a photograph of a significant feature (*shaded area, with arrow marking the camera angle*). Perhaps the most spectacular work is the labyrinth of halls and chambers seen below. Carved into a limestone hill at Hal Saflieni and known as the Hypogeum (from the Greek for "cellar"), it served as a catacomb for some 7,000 dead.

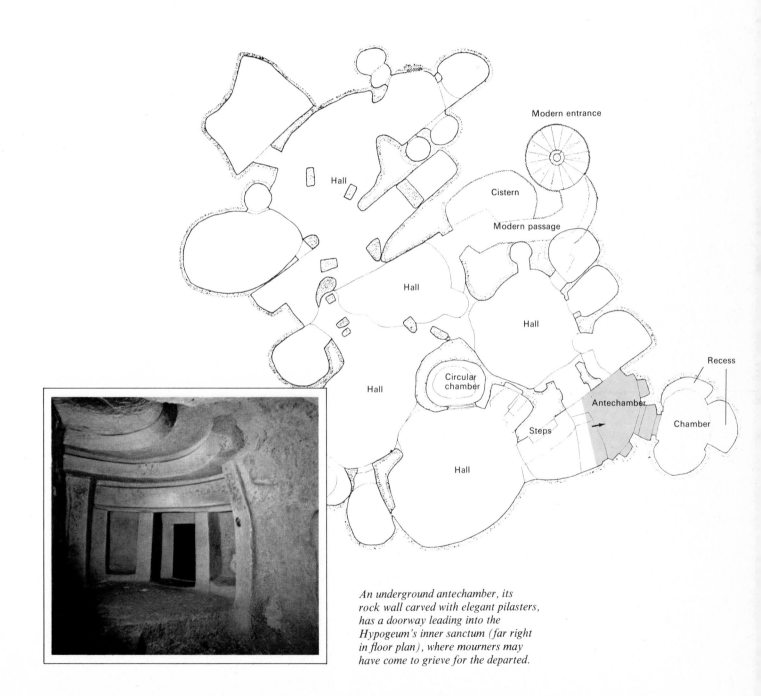

An underground antechamber, its rock wall carved with elegant pilasters, has a doorway leading into the Hypogeum's inner sanctum (far right in floor plan), where mourners may have come to grieve for the departed.

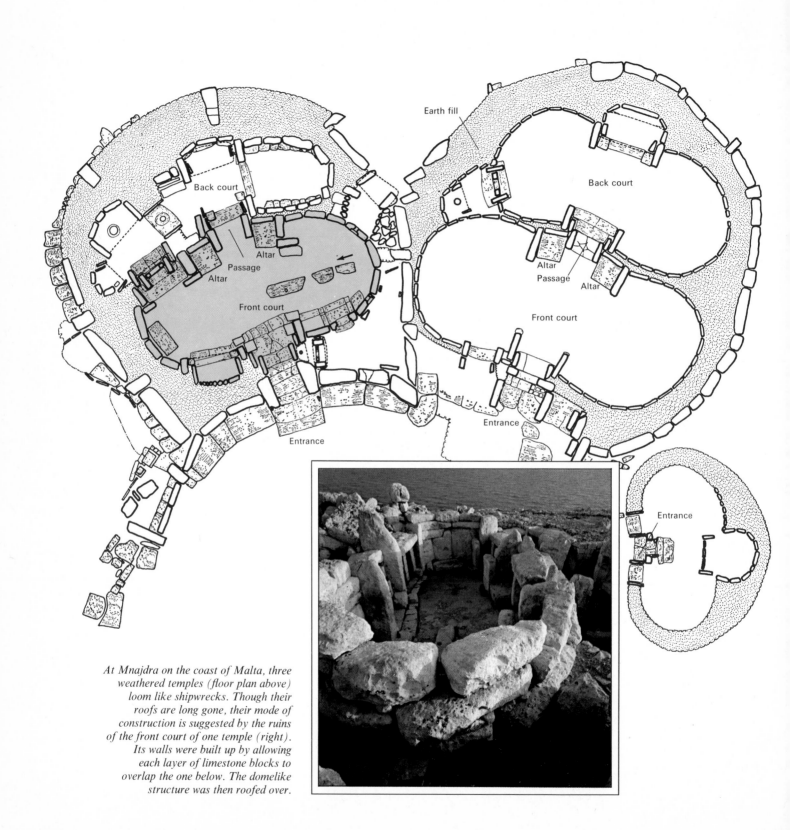

Earth fill

Back court

Back court

Altar

Passage

Altar

Passage

Altar

Front court

Front court

Entrance

Entrance

Entrance

At Mnajdra on the coast of Malta, three weathered temples (floor plan above) loom like shipwrecks. Though their roofs are long gone, their mode of construction is suggested by the ruins of the front court of one temple (right). Its walls were built up by allowing each layer of limestone blocks to overlap the one below. The domelike structure was then roofed over.

A complex of two temples known as the Ggantija (Maltese for "gigantic") adorned the Maltese island of Gozo. The larger temple included three chambers in the shape of a clover leaf (floor plan below) measuring nearly 100 feet across. In the foreground of the biggest chamber (left) the round stones may have been used as a ritual hearth; the table-like structure at rear may have been used in ceremonies, for what purpose is undetermined.

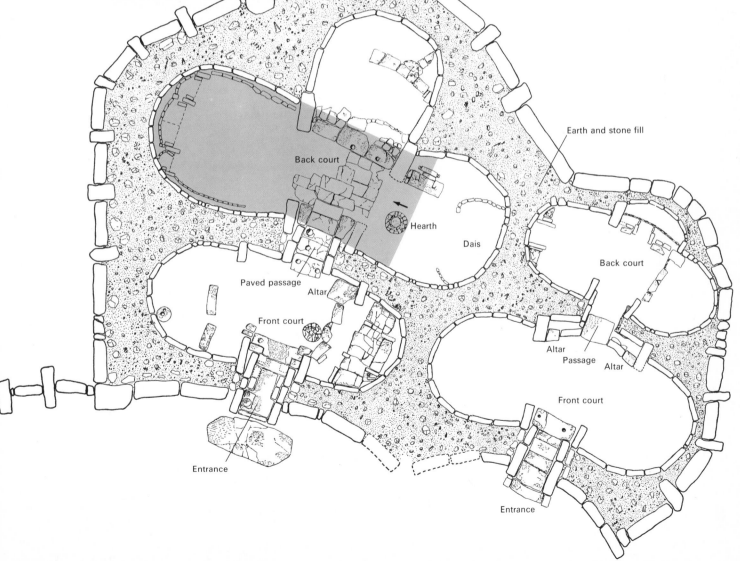

Earth and stone fill

Back court

Hearth

Dais

Back court

Paved passage

Altar

Front court

Altar

Passage

Altar

Front court

Entrance

Entrance

Cut through a limestone block, a doorway less than four feet high (right) opens into a semicircular chamber near the main entrance to the temple complex at Hagar Qim on Malta. The entire monument reflects the builders' skills at their peak. Many interior stones are carefully fitted and decorated. One tremendous slab in the outer wall (lower right in the floor plan) is 22 feet long—the largest single stone in all of Malta's megaliths.

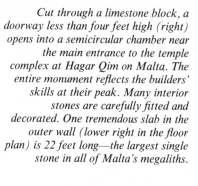

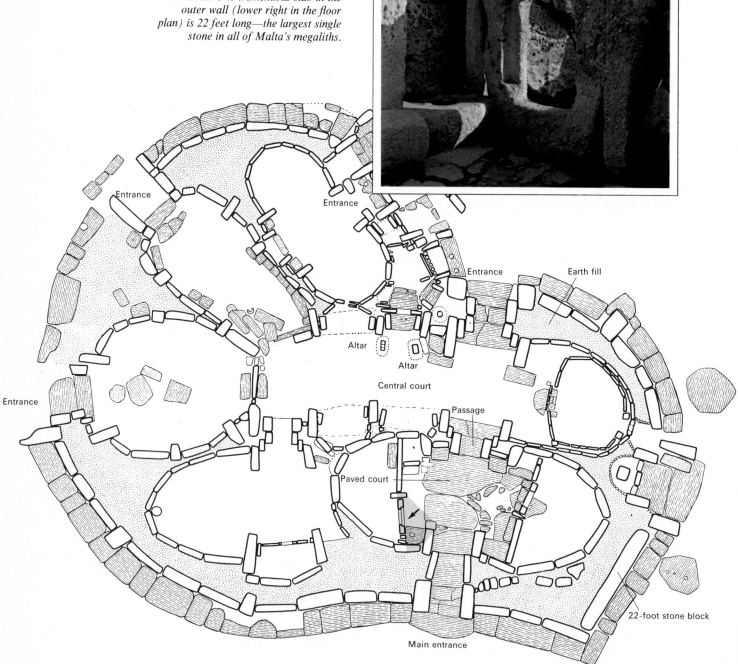

Entrance

Entrance

Entrance

Earth fill

Altar

Altar

Central court

Entrance

Passage

Paved court

22-foot stone block

Main entrance

henge); there are also secret chambers with carved and painted walls, and one opening called the "oracle niche", which echoes when spoken into.

On the second level of the Hypogeum is a small, dark, kidney-shaped room that experts have named the Holy of Holies; red discs are painted on its walls, but in the darkness they could have been apprehended only vaguely by the rare persons allowed to enter. There is no trace of the blackening that would have marked the limestone roof if crowds of worshippers had been permitted to come in with torches.

All the great temples of Malta have the same aura of elaborate mystery. Some are built of smoothly decorated blocks of limestone, like the three temples of Tarxien (discovered in 1913 by a farmer whose plough kept hitting rock). Others are made of rough boulders covered with plaster and red paint. All enclose a profusion of rooms, and the rooms abound in cult objects: statuettes of female figures, altars and hidden closets that still contain the burned remains of sacrificial bulls and rams. Spiral designs like those found in the tombs of northern lands reappear here. There are realistic carvings as well, of rams and pigs and fish. In one room at Tarxien were found some flat stones with five irregularly spaced holes cut through them. Near by are hundreds of round stone balls that would just fit the holes. These may have been "rollers", used for moving blocks around during construction and then discarded. Or, more romantically, ancient priests of Malta may possibly have dropped or rolled the balls towards the holes in a kind of sacred pinball game, and used the results to interpret the will of heaven.

Monuments like Tarxien and Hal Saflieni, like Stonehenge, Avebury and New Grange and the alignments at Carnac, are the summits, the cathedrals of megalithic man's creative achievement. They form only a fraction of his world, however. A complete picture would include southern Sweden and Denmark, where in some regions the stone chamber tombs cluster so thickly—more than 2,000 on the single island of Zealand—that they seem to sprout in every field. It would include the beehive-chambered passage graves of the Orkney Islands; gallery graves like the one at Bagneux in western France, which measures more than 60 feet long, 20 feet wide and 10 feet high, its multiple capstone roof weighing 192 tons; the cemetery of 80 tombs next to a walled town at Los Millares in southern Spain; and the statue-menhirs of Corsica, carved into grotesque human shapes, perhaps as charms against an invading enemy.

All these monuments shared a common fate. For centuries they lorded proudly over the landscape; then, little by little, they were abandoned and their uses forgotten. They grew weather-beaten and overgrown. They were thrown down and shattered by the fury of nature and the equal fury of the Christian church, which considered them sacrilegious. Practical men took away their stones to build bridges and walls. Over centuries of abuse the monuments drifted into oblivion or confused folklore. Only within the recent past have they begun to be admired again and studied, cleaned up and restored.

On the twelfth day of Christmas, 1648, John Aubrey of Wiltshire went riding to hounds with a bibulous party of friends. Galloping past the ghostly grey stones of Avebury, John Aubrey was the first person in hundreds of years to recognize that they formed a pattern that belonged to another age. It reminded him, he said, of a scene "where the Giants fought with great stones against the gods".

Aubrey's merry hunt presaged the era of scientific exploration and examination of the megaliths. Soon they were being uncovered and dug up all over Western Europe. Even then, recognition of their significance was a long time in coming.

It was no secret that man in many places and many ages (to our own day) has felt impelled to erect monuments to major events in his life. The Old Testament patriarch Jacob woke after a dream in which God foretold the glory of his race. He set up a pillar "and poured oil on the top of it. And he called the name of that place Bethel." Joshua set up 12 stones to commemorate the crossing of the river Jordan by the 12 tribes of Israel. Stones of huge size have been found, sometimes in great quantities, in dozens of widely separated places: on the high plateaus of Tibet, in the jungles of Madagascar, in Algeria, Israel, Iran, Korea and on Easter Island in the far Pacific. A Japanese emperor reigning in the Seventh Century A.D. issued a decree forbidding his people to waste valuable time putting up large rock tombs for their ancestors. In parts of Africa and in Assam, on the edge of the Himalayas, giant stones are still being set up to record memorable events in individual or tribal lives.

In the ancient Middle East, notably in Egypt, and in Mycenaean Greece, man also built vast monuments at very early dates on a scale that dazzled later generations. The classical Greeks, for instance, were so impressed by the earlier Mycenaean civilization that they assumed such works were beyond the powers of man. They called them "Cyclopean", built by the Cyclopes, supernatural beings who they believed were rivals of Zeus. Such structures as the arched

The so-called Sleeping Lady, a four-and-a-half-inch terra-cotta sculpture, was found in Hal Saflieni, the vast subterranean tomb complex on Malta. The figure may represent a priestess or a fertility goddess in a deep and dream-filled slumber.

gates of Mycenae and the pyramids and obelisks of Egypt are distinguished from megaliths by the fact that the stones are carefully shaped and polished and smoothly fitted together to form regular outlines.

It was tempting to link the ancient edifices of the Mediterranean world and the monuments of Europe to a common source, and for many experts the megaliths fitted nicely into an East-West diffusion theory of civilization. This theory derives from the demonstrable origin of European agriculture, literacy and urbanism in the Middle East: throughout ancient history Eastern states traded with Europe and at times

attempted to conquer Europe, or at least parts of it. The earliest European civilizations—Greek, Etruscan, Roman—appear in many ways to have derived from the older civilizations of the Middle East and Egypt. Thus scholars developed a "model" of cultural diffusion. They held that cultural innovation in the East and absorption by the West was at the very least a handy explanation, and at the most a standard pattern of history. Moreover, in the absence of any useful dating system except the calendars used by the Eastern civilizations themselves, the appearance of any new cultural manifestation in Europe usually could not be demonstrated to be earlier than some plausible prototype in the Middle East.

So the great-monument idea was believed to have spread west and north along the routes of commerce.

The monuments themselves, as they were imitated successively farther and farther from their cradle, would degenerate more and more from the harmonious structures of the East.

At first it was thought that the tholos tombs of Mycenaean Greece were the obvious prototypes for the passage graves of Western Europe, but by the 1920s it was clear that Mycenae had begun exchanging trade goods with northern and Western Europe in the Early Bronze Age of those areas. Since many, if not most, of the passage graves were evidently pre-Bronze Age, clearly this suggestion was untenable. However, earlier and less spectacular stone-built tombs exist in and around the Aegean, and these were considered by many archaeologists to be the source from which, ultimately, the megalithic tombs of Western Europe derived.

At no time, however, were all the experts content with this theory of Eastern ancestry. For one thing, the megaliths have a very different feel about them from the tombs and temples of Egypt and Greece. Not only are they rougher and cruder, but they appear to have been built to different standards by people who saw the world with different eyes. Aside from bulk, there is little or no formal aesthetic resemblance between the two classes of building. Also, even ardent diffusionists could find no satisfactory Eastern origin for the stone circles, the henge monuments and the alignments of the West. So there have always been voices to insist that the one culture could not simply have diffused into the other.

Recent scientific discoveries indicate that the dissenting voices were right. In the late 1940s an American chemist, Dr. Willard Libby, developed the system of dating ancient organic objects by measuring their content of carbon 14, a radioactive isotope that disintegrates at a fixed rate over thousands of years. All living things absorb carbon 14 from the atmosphere during their lives, but at their death they cease taking it in. So the measurement of organic material—usually charcoal, bone, peat from ancient settlements or burial sites—dates the death of the organism within statistically defined limits (a carbon-14 date is never exact, but always a range, usually of about 100 to 200 years). The first radiocarbon datings of objects buried in megalithic tombs indicated they were older than had been supposed, yet they still could be squeezed into a chronology in which they might have derived from the East. So, initially, the diffusion theory seemed supported.

But by about 1960, carbon-14 datings from megalithic tombs in Brittany indicated that they had been built considerably earlier than 3000 B.C., which made an Eastern origin almost impossible to defend. Moreover, this surprisingly early dating was quite consistent with other carbon-14 dates for the earlier phases of the Neolithic, or Late Stone Age, elsewhere in Europe. A whole new chronological pattern was thus beginning to emerge.

Meanwhile, attempts to correlate the radiocarbon "calendar" with the earliest human calendar—that of ancient Egypt—were running into difficulties. Carefully selecting organic objects from Egyptian tombs that had been dated by interpretation of hieroglyphics, a few radiocarbon laboratories began to discover that the earlier tombs, between about 3000 B.C. and 1000 B.C., did not fit the radiocarbon dates for the objects contained in them.

Searching for an independent source of "known-age" samples, University of Arizona scientists hit upon the bristlecone pine, which lives to great ages high on the slopes of the White Mountains in eastern California. These trees are probably the oldest living things on earth: at least one tree is 4,600 years old, as evidenced by the number of annual growth rings in its trunk. The cool, dry climate in which the bristlecone pines grow inhibits decay, so that trees may survive without rotting for many centuries after they have died. The thickness of the growth rings varies slightly from year to year according to weather conditions, so regular growth patterns can be observed, enabling scientists to correlate the rings from one tree with those of another, provided that the trees have lived for some time in the same environment.

Thus it has been possible to construct, from living and dead bristlecone pine trees, a tree-ring calendar stretching back to about 6000 B.C., and the scientists hope that it may eventually prove possible to reach even further back than this. But equally important is the fact that this calendar can be used to check the carbon-14 calendar. Because each growth ring of a tree lives only for the year in which it grows, it ceases to absorb radiocarbon after one year; so the rings give progressively earlier radiocarbon dates in direct relation to their year of growth. Any of these rings, then, can be carbon-dated; and the two dates—the actual age of the tree ring and its age indicated by carbon dating—can be compared.

Supplied with several bristlecone pine samples by Dr. C. W. Ferguson of the University of Arizona, three radiocarbon laboratories started a series of dating programmes—at the universities of Arizona, Pennsylvania and California at San Diego. These ongoing programmes will provide increasingly refined calibrations for determining the true age of radiocarbon

Text continued on page 33

Carbon 14: Yardstick to Prehistory

The instant a living organism dies, a kind of clock inside it begins to tick. What might be called the moving parts of that clock are atoms of carbon 14, or C-14, and the ticking is their steady disintegration (*overleaf*). Because C-14 is radioactive, it is the crucial element in a technique called radiocarbon dating, which scientists can use to determine when something as old as 40,000 years actually lived, and thus they can put a date to cultures that thrived thousands of years ago—including the monument builders'.

For some time C-14 dating has been suspected of being slightly imprecise. But recently physicists have tracked down the suspected error and have devised a way of correcting radiocarbon readings (*overleaf*). With this new technique, C-14 dating has acquired a new degree of accuracy—and has caused a rewriting of history (*page 32*).

The formation and travels of C-14 molecules, beginning in outer space, are diagrammed in the four panels at right.

1. Cosmic rays from outer space bombard the molecules in the earth's upper atmosphere; as the molecules break apart, nuclear debris—bits of atoms, including protons and neutrons—fly free.

2. A free-floating neutron hits and merges with an atom of nitrogen in the atmosphere; the extra neutron in the nitrogen creates a tension inside it, and in this unstable state the nitrogen ejects one proton. The residue is an atom of C-14.

3. Settling in the atmosphere, the newly formed C-14 atom meets a molecule of oxygen, or O2, which combines with the C-14. The unified molecules of C-14 and O2 (called C14 O2), a kind of carbon dioxide, drift downwards and are absorbed by the earth's water and plants. When an animal eats a plant—or eats another animal that has eaten a plant—it incorporates C-14 into its body. During the animal's lifetime the C-14 in its tissues is constantly disintegrating, but the supply of it is constantly replenished; thus the amount of C-14 in its body remains roughly constant.

4. When the animal dies, the C-14 atoms inside it (*purple dots*) continue to deteriorate—by losing electrons—and no new C-14 atoms replace them. Because this depletion is measurable, the clock has begun to tick.

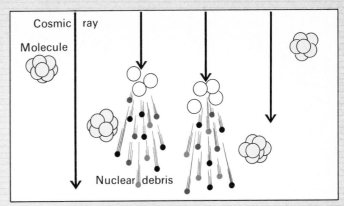

1. **Cosmic rays creating nuclear debris.**

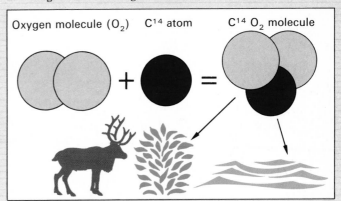

2. **Nitrogen atom becoming C-14 atom.**

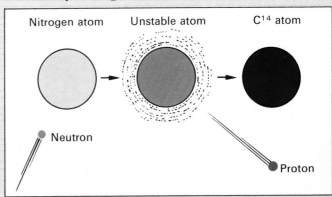

3. **C-14 and oxygen entering live organisms.**

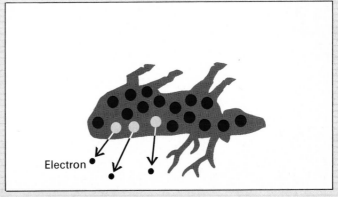

4. **C-14 beginning to deplete.**

The Deterioration of Carbon 14 in a Two-Gramme Sample

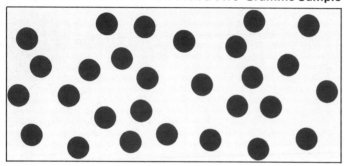

At the moment of death: 28 disintegrations per minute

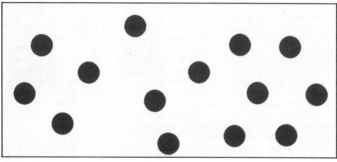

5,730 years after death: 14 disintegrations per minute

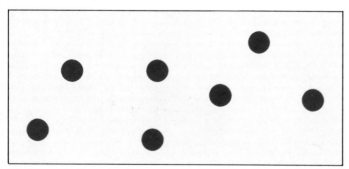

11,460 years after death: seven disintegrations per minute

Correcting the Carbon Clock

Reading the C-14 clock simply involves counting disintegrating molecules with an instrument similar to a Geiger counter. Physicists know that in a two-gramme sample (*panels at left*) of organic matter that has just died, 28 molecules disintegrate in one minute. If the sample died 5,730 years prior to the counting, only 14 disintegrations now register. Every 5,730 years—the span called the half life of C-14—the number diminishes by half. Thus, if the counter records seven disintegrations, the sample is now reckoned to be about 11,460 years old.

The orderliness of this method was deceptively simple and too often the radiocarbon dates became suspect when the object's age could be determined by other means. Some scientists were on the verge of scrapping the technique when a new way of recalibrating radiocarbon dates was found.

The new method involved the bristlecone pine tree—the oldest known living thing on earth, able to survive more than 4,000 years. By counting its rings (*right*) its exact age could be determined. After the ring count, scientists could radiocarbon-date the same tree sample and compare the two readings. Comparisons showed how far off the C-14 dates were—not far in young specimens, but much more so in older ones (*graph at far right*). This set a standard for correcting C-14 dating.

When recalibrated C-14 dates were applied to megalithic monuments, the monuments' position in history was reversed. The erecting of the ancient stones turned out to be far earlier than anyone had thought, long predating the supposedly earlier cultures of Greece and the Middle East.

Dating the Bristlecone Pine

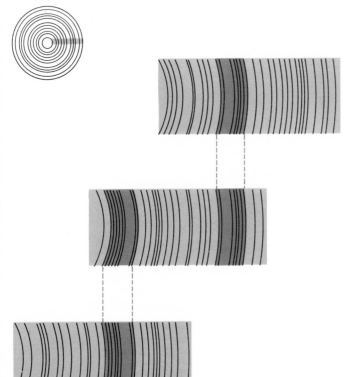

Recalibrating Carbon-14 Dates

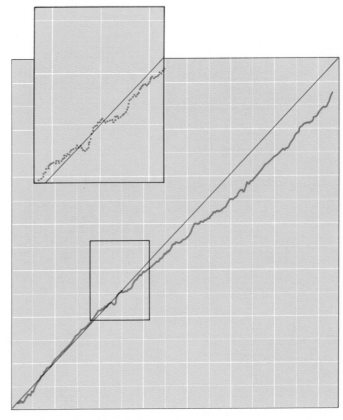

Three bands show how a sample from a live tree helps to date dead ones. The uppermost band —which corresponds to the horizontal bar in the cross section at top—represents a sample from a live tree; each vertical strip in it marks a year's growth. Irregularities in the strips reflect flux in the climate, and any other tree that endured the same conditions shows the same patterns. Thus, samples from dead trees (second and third bands) can be matched with the live one—and the time they lived determined. The sum of many readings from such overlapping samples gave scientists several millennia of dates to use in measuring against radiocarbon dates.

Two lines plotted on a grid—each of whose blocks represents 100 years—show the discrepancies between uncorrected radiocarbon dates and dates corrected according to tree-ring recalibration. The wriggly line—actually a series of connected dots (see inset)—stands for the uncorrected dates of many samples. The straight diagonal is the same sequence after correction. The comparison shows that for younger specimens (lower left) the differences are uneven and not alarmingly great. For older material, however, the discrepancies tend to grow. By the time of the earliest monument builders (upper right), the readings are nearly an entire millennium apart.

Mesolithic Age

Neolithic Age

Copper Age

Bronze Age

Iron Age

Once the carbon-14 dates had been recalibrated, the monuments of Western Europe were proven to be far older than had been assumed. These older dates also reversed a theory of prehistory. Called the Diffusionist Theory, it had postulated that the megaliths owed their origins to the Middle East; and indeed the earlier carbon-14 dates showed the Middle Eastern monuments to be older. But, as this chart demonstrates, the corrected carbon-14 dates prove that most of the European monuments predate or are contemporary with Middle Eastern cultures (below heavy line). England's stone circles, for example, predate all but the Sumerian civilization. Some Breton passage graves are the earliest megaliths of all. And the temples of Malta are the oldest free-standing stone monuments in the world.

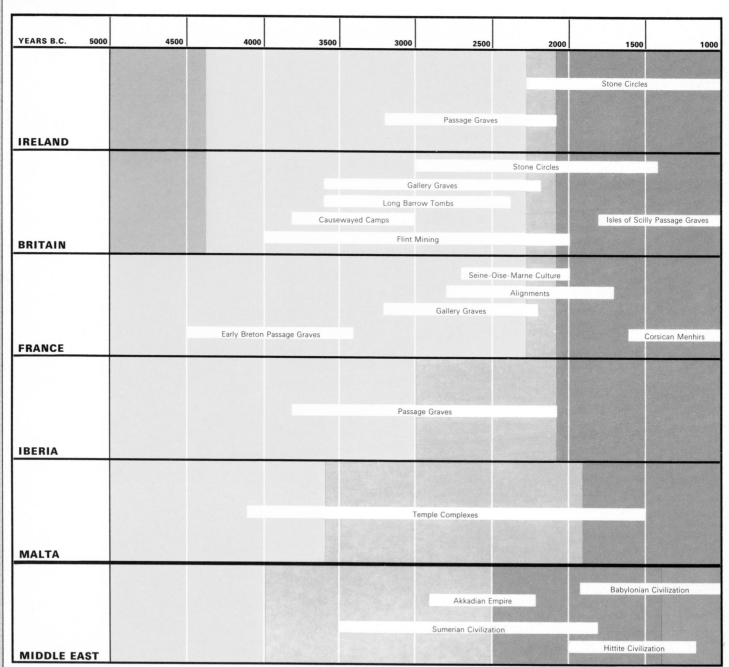

YEARS B.C.   5000   4500   4000   3500   3000   2500   2000   1500   1000

IRELAND
- Stone Circles
- Passage Graves

BRITAIN
- Stone Circles
- Gallery Graves
- Long Barrow Tombs
- Causewayed Camps
- Isles of Scilly Passage Graves
- Flint Mining

FRANCE
- Seine-Oise-Marne Culture
- Alignments
- Gallery Graves
- Early Breton Passage Graves
- Corsican Menhirs

IBERIA
- Passage Graves

MALTA
- Temple Complexes

MIDDLE EAST
- Babylonian Civilization
- Akkadian Empire
- Sumerian Civilization
- Hittite Civilization

dates. But by 1967 the scientists felt that sufficient work had been done, with consistent results among the three laboratories, to propose a tentative recalibration of radiocarbon chronology.

Their results show that Dr. Libby's original calculation was an approximation and that radiocarbon dates may vary considerably from the true age of a sample, most probably because the amount of radiocarbon in the atmosphere has varied somewhat from time to time. From about 1000 B.C., going backwards in time, the age of the bristlecone pine samples, as dated by their own growth rings, became gradually older and older than the radiocarbon dates. (This supported the Egyptian calendar dates that had also appeared to be older than the contemporaneous samples as dated by the radiocarbon method.)

As far as can be determined, the uncorrected radiocarbon dates of around 2000 B.C. should be recalibrated to about 2500 B.C.; dates of about 2500 B.C. should be recalibrated to about 3200 and so on. Of course, more work on the "known-age" programme will continue to refine the recalibration calculations, but the general pattern is sufficiently consistent already to indicate that revisions in the future will not be of any great magnitude.

Thus there now seems no chance that the megaliths can have derived from the Middle East or the Aegean. Some passage graves in Brittany date to about 4800 B.C., and the earliest Maltese temples go back to 4500 B.C. The builders of Western Europe were creating their monuments of stone when the Egyptians were still building in perishable wood and clay. No longer can the megalith builders be written off as awkward imitators of higher cultures. Apparently they created an independent culture quite their own, and they did it far from the cradles of the East.

For all the search and study that has gone into the subject, tantalizingly little is known for certain about the people who built the megaliths. What is clear, however, is that these people were moved by an overwhelming drive to band together repeatedly over many centuries, abandoning their daily pursuits to put forth colossal communal effort. It must have been some kind of spiritual urge, perhaps not unlike the inspiration that thousands of years later led Christians of the Middle Ages to cover much of the same land with a mantle of Gothic churches.

Why did they do it? Why mobilize the bulk of their labour force for years of backbreaking effort that promised no material reward? Why indulge in such extravagant expenditures of energy at a time when there were few or no luxuries in daily life? Was there a hunger in megalithic man, as we often see in 20th Century man, for permanence?

There is no certain answer. For all their skills, the megalith builders left no written records. Their religious secrets, engineering formulas, traditions and taboos, their family and social structures, all were passed from generation to generation by word of mouth and committed to memory. As far as we know the memory died out before any of their descendants had acquired the art of writing. Whatever message they had to leave behind them endures in their stones and in their graves.

Nevertheless the stones are there, unique in the world, and they represent a turning point in the long journey of the human race when, after millennia of being little more than minor participants in the natural process, men were increasingly shaping nature to their own intellectual and spiritual ends.

Identifying those ends is a problem no less challenging for being continually posed in different terms. The archaeologist Jacquetta Hawkes has said that "every age has the Stonehenge it deserves—or desires", one built more or less in its own image. In the classicist 17th Century, England's first great architect, Inigo Jones, came to Stonehenge and "saw" a Roman temple, which he set down on paper, smooth, serene and symmetrical. In the romantic 19th Century, Stonehenge was seen as a dark and bloody precinct (one large stone near the entrance was baptized the Slaughter Stone), and engravings of the period emphasize and exaggerate the unevenness of the stones. And now, in the 20th Century, mathematicians and astronomers speculate that Stonehenge may have been the first computer.

The search will go on. New visions and new theories will arise as long as the stones remain and there are men and women to be fascinated by them. In the meantime the patient labours of thousands of professional archaeologists proceed at an increased pace, adding continually to our store of information. Gradually the museums accumulate fragmentary remains, bones and artifacts. Prehistoric garbage dumps reveal what megalithic man ate. Impressions of seeds baked into clay pots tell what crops he raised.

People who have gone on living in the Stone Age, like the Kwakiutl Indians of the Northwest Coast in the 19th Century and the Trobriand Islanders in the 20th Century, have been carefully studied, and sometimes their codes and customs can be extrapolated into the distant past. In some megalithic tombs, for example, the bones of the last persons to be buried are formally laid out, while the older ones are swept unceremoniously into a corner. Among some primitive peoples of modern times a similar practice obtains. They explain it by saying that they fear the dead as long as flesh adheres to the bones, but when it is all rotted away the skeleton is only so much rubbish. But any parallels between the two epochs must be made carefully: the primitive cultures of today have had thousands of years in which to change since the time of megalithic man.

More reliable information can sometimes be found by analysing the deepest, most primitive strands in ancient stories preserved in inscriptions or in books of the Hebrews and Greeks and Egyptians. Myths and fairy tales often contain recollections left over from a forgotten past. Turns of phrase and superstitions current today can perhaps be traced back to religious or magical rituals of the Stone Age.

Using all such sources of information, it is possible to make a tentative plunge into the past, as in the chapter that follows. With what is now known, complemented by some educated guesswork, one can go back several thousand years to primeval Europe and share in the stirrings of the new life there, to an epoch when man for the first time in his career felt capable of building great monuments designed to defy time and outlast his own small life span on earth.

Monuments to Patient Zeal

Like the towering cathedrals of the Middle Ages, Europe's greatest prehistoric monuments bespeak religion in more ways than one. Some were specifically religious; others furthered man's knowledge. All were prodigious public works, and the mere act of building them expressed a deep dedication akin to religious zeal.

It took centuries to complete the temples at Tarxien on Malta. It took countless workers to build the passage grave at New Grange in Ireland (*below*). And in Brittany, amid mile-long rows of menhirs, small groups of men may have studied the moon with the same devotion that went into the building of their alignments.

Skilled and devoted, a stone carver chisels spiral designs on a huge curbstone, placed across the door to the New Grange tomb.

Gifts for the Dead at the Shrine of a Fertility Goddess

In a paved courtyard of the temple complex at Tarxien on the island of Malta, a priest lays the bones of a sacrificed goat on an altar. Behind him two priestesses bring bowls containing food and drink. Above them all looms the ponderous, eight-foot-high statue of an ample goddess.

The artist's rendition is imaginary yet true to fact. Although very little is known about the religion of the prehistoric Maltese, the immense ruins of their west temple at Tarxien have yielded up a flint knife, some charred goat bones and fragments of a colossal statue, identifiable as the goddess of fertility. These and other finds indicate that the Maltese not only believed in the life-giving goddess of fertility, but also combined her worship with a cult of dead ancestors, many of whom were buried near by and would presumably enjoy frequent gifts of food and drink.

So it is possible to visualize the end of the sombre ceremony. The priest places the goat bones in a niche behind the altar, along with the sacrificial knife. Then he uses a stone plug to seal in the relics—in exactly the place where archaeologists found them 2,500 years later.

In stately procession a priest and two priestesses place food and drink and the charred bones of a sacrificial goat on an altar in the west temple of Tarxien. The goat was consumed by flames in the ceremonial hearth in the foreground.

Plotting the Moon's Path in a Panorama of Upright Stones

More than 4,500 years ago, monument builders in Brittany transformed the countryside around Carnac into a surreal landscape of thousands of stones, stretching for miles in nearly parallel rows, 10 or more abreast. These immense alignments were once thought to have been built as funeral procession ways, but they are now considered a kind of giant graph paper used by skilled astronomers to study the movements of celestial bodies.

At least that is the theory recently proposed by the Scottish engineering professor Alexander Thom, who based his conclusions on extensive surveys and computations. If Thom is correct, the alignments provided prehistoric observers with astronomical information that was not to be rediscovered until the 16th Century A.D.

In the reconstruction at right, three astronomers are using the Le Menec alignment to measure off their sighting lines and determine the details of the moon's movements as it approaches its northernmost rising position. By means of such complex calculations they discovered that there is an 18.6-year cycle of the moon, and they used this information to predict the frequency of eclipses.

Using the alignments of stones at Carnac like a gigantic sheet of graph paper, neolithic astronomers stretch out two predetermined lengths of oxhide rope as measuring tapes to help them plot their sightings of the rising moon.

Rites of Summer in the Inner Circle of Sarsens

As seen from the inner circle at Stonehenge, the sun rises over the Heel Stone at the time of the summer solstice. This dramatic fact has triggered the theory that Stonehenge was built as an observatory. It has also inspired intriguing speculation—illustrated at right—about the ancient ceremony held at that time.

What did this putative ceremony represent? Since the builders owed their livelihood to farming, they undoubtedly believed in a fertility cult and offered rites to ensure abundance in crops and animals.

The site itself supports some reasonable deductions about the celebrants. The ponderous sarsen stones that ring Stonehenge's inner circle must have required hundreds of men to transport and erect them. Thus there must have been a large local population, too large to be accommodated inside a ring that is only 97 feet in diameter. This suggests the existence of some criterion of rank for admission into the inner circle. Perhaps, as shown here, this select area was reserved for priests and chieftains, while the great majority of the populace watched agape from the crowded plain beyond.

The dramatic moment of the year arrives as the summer solstice sun rises over the Heel Stone at Stonehenge. Inside the great inner circle of sarsens, priests salute the sunrise, hoping it portends another season of abundance.

Chapter Two: Myth and Magic at Stonehenge

A sceptre of polished limestone, inlaid with a pattern of bone, and a copper dagger exemplify the skill of craftsmen in southern England between 2100 and 1500 B.C. Found in the graves of warriors, both objects probably served as ceremonial symbols of authority, rather than as weapons in combat.

It is Midsummer Eve, the shortest night of the year, sometime in the middle of the Second Millennium B.C. Let us re-create the scene.

Thousands of men, women and children from local tribes and distant lands have been converging for days on Salisbury Plain. Dressed in the finest leather cloaks and linen kilts, powdered and painted, they come decked out in ancient ornaments made of boar tusk and the latest continental fashion, turquoise from Brittany. The wealthier people among them also sport gold pins, beads, belt toggles, amulets and daggers of bronze. They come padding on bare feet or leather sandals through the forest paths, across the hillside pastures and through the tangled thickets of the river bottoms.

Ordinary life is at a standstill: grain grows high in the fields, the cattle browse, swine root leisurely through the uncrowded expanse of virgin forest. Workers in the flint mines have put down their tools. Bronze workers who have been toiling in their smithies have left their fires; potters have covered their clay and banked their kilns. Hunter and fisherman, sailor and merchant, mason, chieftain and priest, all are trekking with their families to appropriate places to take part in the night's ceremonies. The most prestigious and imposing of such places in their world is here at Stonehenge.

This night is important because it marks a yearly crisis, a turning point in the life of the heavens. The sun is at the zenith of its power. For six months the point at which it rises on the horizon has been creeping northwards. Now it is about the slip back into a long decline, weakening to the south until the moment of rebirth in midwinter.

Such a moment is a crisis, too, in the life of man.

His well-being depends on the orderly procession of the sun through its traditional paths. He too has a traditional path to walk and gestures to make in order to establish his communion and kinship with the powers that control the rhythms of heaven and earth.

Thus tonight will be an outpouring of the concentrated energy and faith of the people, their noisiest animal spirits and deepest spiritual longings. It will be a combination of religious ritual, commercial fair and dramatic spectacle, all carried on simultaneously. For the time is still far distant when these varied forms of human expression will be considered separate and incompatible.

At Stonehenge a particular local feeling intensifies the ceremony. The people take pride in the monument itself. In part they are celebrating the lofty ambitions and prodigious skills of their ancestors, who built and rebuilt this stupendous shrine for more than a thousand years. Various generations have made it a point of honour to bring something new to improve or beautify the scene. Material conditions of life have changed over the centuries; new tools and materials and techniques have been imported from overseas or developed on the spot. But every Midsummer Night for over a millennium the throngs have gathered this way to perform these motions and express these same hopes and fears.

Nothing in the world, as far as these people can imagine the world, compares with Stonehenge. They have perhaps been to visit larger and more awesome monuments, like the ancient circles at Avebury over the hills to the north, or even the endless stone rows across the channel in Brittany. But none of these others can match the grandeur and the architectural unity of Stonehenge.

In the crowd there may be traders from across the sea—from perhaps as far away as the Mediterranean —who have come all this distance to trade bronze daggers and other luxury goods for the raw mineral wealth of Britain. They are familiar with great buildings in their homelands and have seen other stone monuments in their travels. Yet Stonehenge will awe them too. The stones are as big, if not as smooth, as any that went into the fabled walls and sumptuous palaces of the East. There are no palaces here, or oppressive kings or pharaohs to dwell in them; no standing army or class of bureaucrats. Nothing but what to the sophisticated traveller's eye looks like clans of simple primitives who live in villages of flimsy huts and who seem to be ignorant of most of the civilized arts that are flourishing elsewhere.

For all that, these are no savages. Since their Stone Age ancestors first chose this spot and laid out the first of the shrines that have stood here, they have grown rich and powerful. Their territory stands at a major crossroads of trade through which amber obtained from the North Sea coast, gold from Ireland and tin from Cornwall are funnelled to the ports from which ships take them to the inexhaustible markets of the Mediterranean. Profiting from this strategic position, the local chieftains have acquired wealth and prestige. Tonight they can be seen swaggering about resplendent in all the finery they can afford, flashing weapons and ornaments of bronze and gold that will one day be buried with them.

The round mounds that cover the tombs of many such stalwarts lie dotted over the plain alongside longer barrows where whole families were buried in the old days. All are made of the white chalk that underlies the ground in this region. Some are overgrown with grass. Those that still stand uncovered look a ghostly grey now by the light of the moon and flicker with the shadows from a hundred fires.

The bonfires blaze on hilltop and plain as they have done on this night as far back as memory goes, and as they will still blaze for thousands of years in the future in Europe when the celebration will come to be known as St. John's Eve. Then as now, the young men and women will dance the night through, weaving in and out among the fires, running and kicking and bounding high over the flames. Throughout the night the exuberance goes on: wild leaping, dancing, chanting, random and passionate coupling in the shadows. All is revel and license. At the same time all is traditional and holy.

Man has performed such mingled rites and revels almost since he began to be aware of his identity. Like the upright stones themselves, the leaps and dances are symbolic gestures, pounding out a message to the beat of drums and stamping feet, stimulating Mother Earth to fecundity. The higher the leaps, the more vigorous the embraces and the wilder the dance, the more assurance there is that the tides of life will flow bountifully in the year to come. The grain will sprout, the game will swarm, the fish will run, there will be bumper crops of calves and pigs and newborn human babes.

Fresh logs keep the flames roaring. From hilltop to hilltop additional bonfires and beacons take up the signal. If the night is clear they can be seen blazing for a hundred miles and more.

Only at the approach of dawn do the fires begin to die. As the sky lightens in the northeast, the scattered mass of celebrants begins to move inward towards the monument, whose thick grey pillars have

The English antiquarian William Stukeley drew this reconstruction of prehistoric Avebury in 1723. The circles at the top (marked "Abury") are visible today; the serpentine avenues leading from them have disappeared.

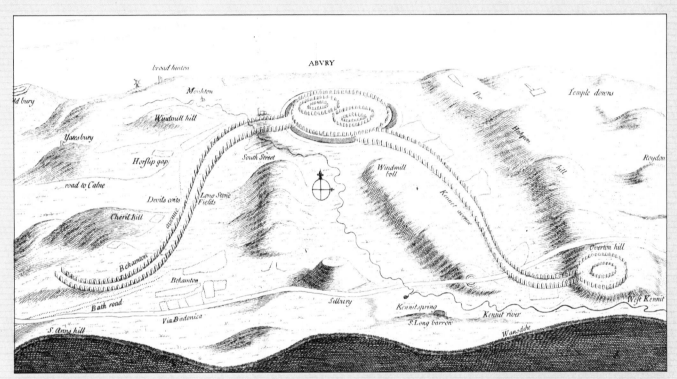

been looking down on the festivities. The pillars as they stand represent the latest advance in architectural sophistication, but they contain elements that go back to a more primitive past. The wise men —priests or seers—who are the guardians of the traditions of the people number among the secrets that they have committed to memory all the transformations that Stonehenge has undergone. As they precede the celebrants up the broad way that leads into the monument, it is as if they were treading out the history of the race.

The way to the centre of the shrine follows a wide, grassy avenue bordered by ditches and banks. This avenue was smoothed out more than 1,000 years ago; it was then widened and shifted to the east when the alignment of the stones in the circle was altered several centuries later. Rising some 16 feet near the middle of the Avenue is a burly marker, a natural boulder, unshaped and unpolished, weighing at least 35 tons. This is probably the oldest of all the big stones that have been brought to this site. In a much later day it will be called the Heel Stone (apparently because of an idle tale of the devil throwing the stone at a friar and hitting him on the heel, which left an imprint on its surface). When the first monument was built there—the one archaeologists of modern times will call Stonehenge I—the Heel Stone was its most imposing feature, and it had a fittingly important rôle to play in the rites.

Past the Heel Stone, two upright stones stand in the Avenue, one set several feet in front of the other. Beyond them, at the opening in the earthen circle, rises a great symbolic gate, once probably flanked by posts of wood but now by two pillars of stone. The two stones, which are each 16 feet high, are set only a foot and a half apart. The principal entrance is around and past these pillars, through a circular ditch and embankment, enclosing a space of about an acre. This has been holy ground since the construction of Stonehenge I in 2775 B.C. The embankment itself, now carpeted with grass, was originally formed by chalk dug out of the ditch that runs just outside it. Rising six feet on a base 20 feet wide, catching the light of the falling fires and the rising dawn, the embankment effectively shuts off the outside world from the sacred precinct where the night's ceremonies will finally reach their climax.

Gate and Heel Stone were not placed at random. Standing at the centre of the area marked off by the high chalk palisade, looking out through the gate and across the stone, a man could see the sun rise on the morning of the summer solstice, the longest day of the year. Turning at right angles, he would face the spot where it rises at the winter solstice, the shortest day. Located a few miles north or south, these points would no longer be at right angles. The choice of the site argues that those distant ancestors were already wise in the ways of the heavens.

Such precision must have involved scores or even hundreds of years of careful observation, of eye-straining vigils to catch risings and settings through the foggy English air. Such observations have been continued steadily over the centuries by the wise men or priests like those who are today leading the pro-cession. On their calculations of the procession of the seasons, the phases of the moon, tides, eclipses depends much of the safety of the people. From the priests' celestial calendar they learn when to plant their seed and breed their cattle and set out on the treacherous seas.

The embankment's outer sections are marked in the fading shadows by a series of round depressions. (In time, these will be named the Aubrey Holes, for the man who will rediscover them more than 3,000 years in the future.) Originally the holes were 30 to 70 inches in diameter, and dug to an average depth of two and a half feet. There are 56 of them in all, set in a circle at regular intervals of about 16 feet. They were dug and consecrated when the embankment was first built—perhaps as part of the ritual of an earth-orientated faith. Then they were filled to the brim with white chalk. Twice thereafter, in ceremonies whose usage has died out and whose meaning has been forgotten by all but the most learned, they were partly dug up again and refilled. This time the remains of cremated human beings were packed into them, along with fragments of pottery, tools and sundry memorials of daily life.

Touching the now-faint circle of these holes are four standing pillars called the Station Stones. Each is encircled by a ditch about 50 feet in diameter, and together they form the corners of a rough rectangle that is full of recondite meaning, the product of extensive observations and researches into the movements of the heavenly bodies. Lines drawn along the sides of the rectangle or diagonally across it point to risings of the sun and of the moon at both midwinter and midsummer solstices and at the spring and autumn equinoxes as well.

Proceeding towards the centre of Stonehenge, the celebrants pass two noticeably irregular circles of partly silted-up holes (Y and Z holes in 20th Century terminology). These are the remains of a design that was recently begun and then abandoned. The stone uprights intended for them were never set in the holes, although some blue chips were ceremonially placed in their bottoms. Thus nothing obstructs the view of the central pile, the latest and greatest monument of the age.

These central stones, just now taking on the rosy touch of dawn, form a compact whole. But it is easy for those learned in the traditions of the people to see that two separate sets of materials were used in building them, answering to different conceptions and changed more than once in place and shape to meet new requirements of the architects. Of the several dozen stones that form the centre monument, somewhat over half are notably smaller and less harmoniously shaped than the others and are streaked with bluish tints. (These will be called the bluestones by 20th Century archaeologists.)

It was several centuries after the completion of Stonehenge I with its chalk embankment that a more prosperous community with a somewhat different religious bent decided to enhance the monument, first by building rings of bluestones at its centre, then by moving the axis of its great circle to the east to align it with the rising of the midsummer sun. Their endeavours constituted Stonehenge II. Weighing up to five tons apiece, the bluestones were set up in two concentric circles. An opening to the northeast led again to the Heel Stone, for, though there were minor variations in centring the circles, the plan of Stonehenge II was basically the same as the one for

Stonehenge I, orientated approximately towards the midsummer sunrise. And at this time the Avenue was widened from its original 35 to its present 40 feet.

The double circle of bluestones was never completed. Instead, sometime near the end of the Third Millennium, it was dismantled to make way for a still more grandiose conception. For this design, Stonehenge III, a new generation of builders dragged 81 great blocks of sarsen stone from the Marlborough Downs some 20 miles to the north and set them up in two alignments, which have formed the heart of the shrine ever since. There is an outer rim formed by a circle of 30 upright stones, spaced a little more than three feet apart and weighing an average of 26 tons apiece. Each upright supports a flat stone a quarter of its own weight. The edges of these 30 horizontals are artfully grooved and ridged to fit together. Thus they form a continuous circular lintel almost 20 feet off the ground.

By itself, this mighty circle would make the most imposing monument in Europe if not the world. But it is only a prelude to the still more gigantic construction within. Arranged in a horseshoe at the epicentre of Stonehenge are five trilithons, gatelike structures composed of two uprights with a crosspiece. The trilithons increase in height towards the centre of the horseshoe; and it is towards this marvel of construction, stones of up to 50 tons rising to two dozen feet in the air, that all eyes will turn at the peak of this night's ceremonies.

The building of Stonehenge has not stopped with the erection of the sarsens. Like a living organism, it has grown and changed over the intervening years. Seventeen of the old bluestones from the original in-

Four Stages in the Growth of Stonehenge

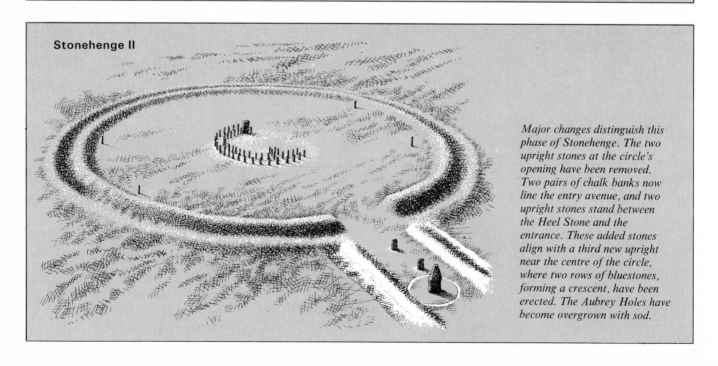

Stonehenge I

The monument's perimeter is permanently defined by chalk banks on either side of a circular trough (see pages 120-121). Just within the inner bank were dug the 56 Aubrey Holes (so named for their discoverer), whose purpose is still debated. The positions of four station posts, possibly for astronomical sightings, have been marked with wooden uprights. Upright stones flank the circle's entrance; the Heel Stone is outside the ring, and near it four posts support the lintel of a wooden gateway.

Stonehenge II

Major changes distinguish this phase of Stonehenge. The two upright stones at the circle's opening have been removed. Two pairs of chalk banks now line the entry avenue, and two upright stones stand between the Heel Stone and the entrance. These added stones align with a third new upright near the centre of the circle, where two rows of bluestones, forming a crescent, have been erected. The Aubrey Holes have become overgrown with sod.

The building of Stonehenge was accomplished not in a single year or a single lifetime but over a span of 1,200 or more years. The builders were not one people but a series of peoples who succeeded one another in southern England. Their methods and materials varied—as much as did their visions of how Stonehenge should look—but they shared a common purpose: to build the most awesome and durable of monuments, and one that may have helped them gain information about the heavens (*pages 114-115*).

Archaeologists divide Stonehenge's construction into four phases, dating the start of the first at about 2750 B.C. After the initial work, the next three phases saw the erection and rearrangement of the stones that still give it its distinctive character. The illustrations on these pages show how Stonehenge may have looked at the end of each of the four phases.

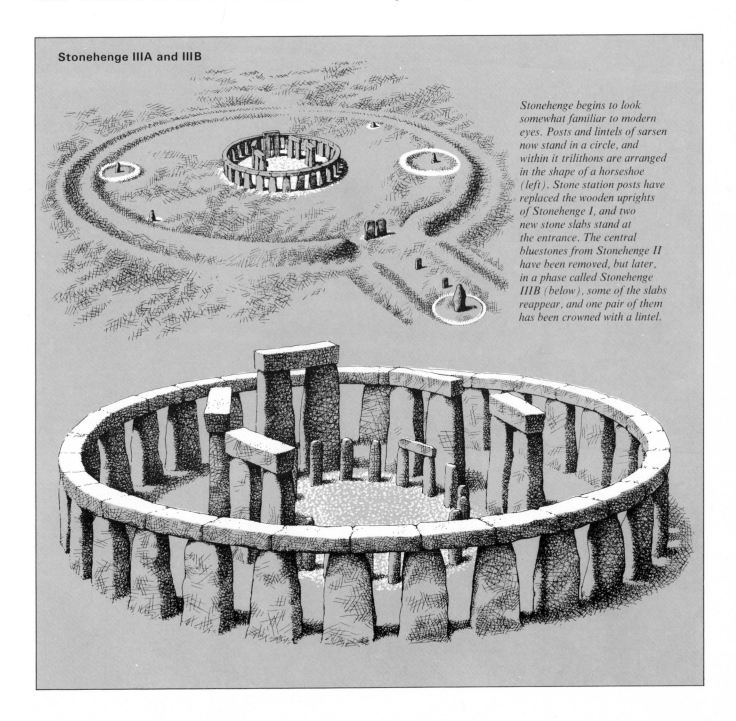

Stonehenge IIIA and IIIB

Stonehenge begins to look somewhat familiar to modern eyes. Posts and lintels of sarsen now stand in a circle, and within it trilithons are arranged in the shape of a horseshoe (left). Stone station posts have replaced the wooden uprights of Stonehenge I, and two new stone slabs stand at the entrance. The central bluestones from Stonehenge II have been removed, but later, in a phase called Stonehenge IIIB (below), some of the slabs reappear, and one pair of them has been crowned with a lintel.

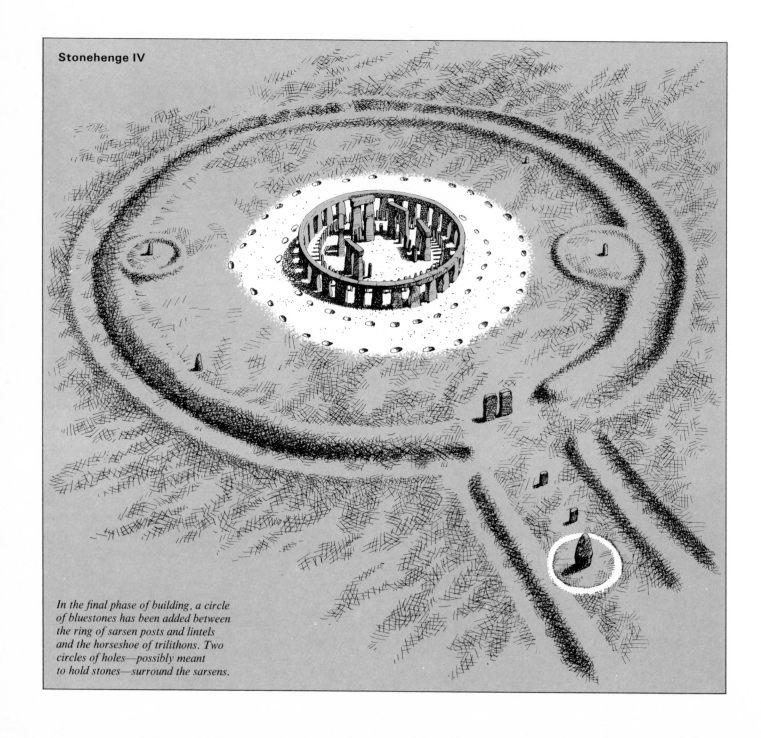

Stonehenge IV

*In the final phase of building, a circle
of bluestones has been added between
the ring of sarsen posts and lintels
and the horseshoe of trilithons. Two
circles of holes—possibly meant
to hold stones—surround the sarsens.*

complete double circle have been carved, polished and set up in an oval cluster of uprights within the Sarsen Circle. Two other bluestones have been placed on top of four of the uprights, forming lintels. Then at a later date these constructions were dismantled and the 19 stones set upright in the shape of a horseshoe. Other bluestones were, at this time or perhaps later, arranged in an irregular circle between the outer Sarsen Circle and the Sarsen Horseshoe.

The astronomical or religious or architectural refinements involved in these various transformations may be of interest only to the most learned of the celebrants. But everyone in the crowd flocking towards the centre of the shrine is aware in some way that centuries of labour, the dreams and sweat of uncounted generations, are involved in tonight's ritual. An act of profound significance is about to occur. No matter that it has occurred at this same time last year and all the years before that; endless repetition cannot deprive the scene of its awful splendour. Indeed the repetition is wonderful and necessary, for it is by repeated gestures in customary surroundings that man can guarantee that he will share in the orderly processes of nature.

This stone structure, made by man but on the immense scale of nature itself, is somehow connected with these orderly processes. All its combined complexity of ditch, bank, pit and stone is hinged on that one point on the northeastern horizon, where—if it turns out that the wise men have calculated correctly, if the ceremonies of the night have been performed in the old and seemly ways, if the bridges of communication between the seen and the unseen worlds have been kept open—the sun will rise to signal that the world will continue in its orderly and life-giving way for another year.

As the sky turns blue and the landscape brightens, the priests raise their arms in silence to invoke the godhead. Sure enough, at that precise instant, looking down through the narrow aperture of the central trilithon past the pillars of the gate, they can see the full disc of the sun climb over the horizon, balance at the edge of the Heel Stone, dance there a moment and then pass on.

Once again, all is right with the world. The clear light of midsummer morning licks up the mists from the meadows, and the assembled people begin to disperse, trudging confidently back to their herds and farms and daily labours for another year.

A scene like the one sketched above might be accepted as plausible by archaeologists in the light of current research and knowledge. This is not to say that there are aspects of it that cannot be challenged. There is, as a matter of fact, hardly anything connected with Stonehenge and megalithic monuments in general that some authority has not called into question for one reason or another. One theory or interpretation may win a degree of acceptance for a time, only to be knocked down when an iconoclast arises, armed with new laboratory tests or reappraisals of old evidence.

No idea, for example, seemed more firmly fixed in the literature than the one asserting that the bluestones of Stonehenge were brought by sea and land from southwest Wales. Fifty years ago a British geologist, Herbert Thomas, demonstrated to almost everyone's satisfaction that the only place on the earth's surface where rocks of their particular de-

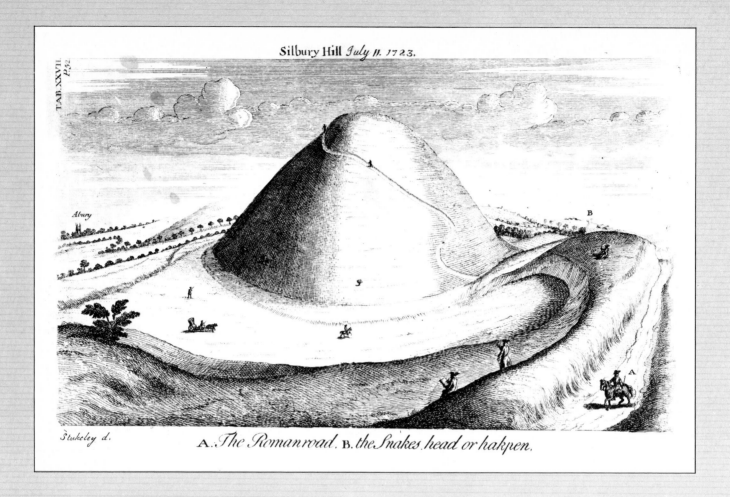

TAB. XXVII. p. 132

Silbury Hill *July 11. 1723.*

Abury

B

A

Stukeley d.

A. *The Roman road.* B. *the Snakes head or hakpen.*

scription (five kinds of blue-tinged stone) are found in conjunction is on the slopes of the Prescelly Mountains 135 miles away in Pembrokeshire.

The assumption that the stones did come from there became the foundation for several complex theories, some of which found their way into the conventionally accepted lore of Stonehenge. Obviously stones brought from so great a distance had to be stones that had special mystico-magical powers. The Prescelly Mountains must have been the centre of a cult, perhaps the abode of a divinity—an earth goddess or moon goddess—recognized as paramount over a large region of Britain. Later, when the stones sacred to that divinity were taken down and battered and rearranged in a subordinate position at Stonehenge, it seemed possible that there had been a religious upheaval. Perhaps a new divinity, a sun god from the East, had been brought to Britain by some

warrior immigrants who defeated and humbled the worshippers of the older divinity.

Another, older theory claimed that the bluestones had been moved long distances not by men but by glaciers. A British geologist, J. W. Judd, suggested in 1902 that the stones had come down from the north on the ice sheets. The theory was abandoned when subsequent study indicated that the ice had not flowed in a southerly direction after all. Another British geologist, G. A. Kellaway, has proposed a different theory, suggesting that the bluestones may have been outcroppings at the bottom of the Bristol Channel that were scooped up by a glacier in the last ice age, then carried eastwards and finally dropped by the receding ice on Salisbury Plain. There the architects of Stonehenge II would have been able to find them, only a few miles from their eventual building site.

Other British geologists give little or no support to

Antiquarian William Stukeley's drawing of Silbury Hill emphasized its 130-foot height, dwarfing the near-by hills he called "Snake's head or hakpen". Stukeley believed the mound was the burial place of Stonehenge's grand Druid priest, but the excavations have disclosed no human remains.

this theory. But whatever the origin of the bluestones may have been, the achievement of the builders was astonishing—the bluestones weigh up to five tons and it was no light task to move them any distance at all. Even if the stones did come from Wales, it is possible that they may not have been brought directly to Stonehenge but were used elsewhere first. Bluestone chips discovered at Silbury Hill 17 miles from the monument and assigned a recalibrated radiocarbon date of between 2700 and 2500 B.C., very close to the time Stonehenge I was built and well before the start of the Bluestone Circle at Stonehenge II, hint that the stones may have stood there before being moved later to their present location.

The presence of traders from the Mediterranean at Stonehenge has been generally accepted in part because of the discovery in some of the local tombs of segmented faience beads, an ornament manufactured in large quantities in Egypt since predynastic times. But now these beads have been subjected to improved chemical and statistical analysis, which indicates that their composition differs significantly from beads found in Egypt. They may have been manufactured in central Europe. They may even have been made in Britain—perhaps in Scotland. Since these minuscule objects (they typically measure only about one-sixteenth of an inch across) form a major part of the material evidence for the existence of a direct link between the builders of Stonehenge and the ancient East, a whole theoretical structure is endangered if it is accepted that the beads were in fact manufactured in Britain.

Since the day in 1740 when the Reverend Dr. William Stukeley observed that "the principle line of the whole work [at Stonehenge points to] the Northeast,

whereabouts the sun rises when the days are longest," it has been widely agreed that astronomical alignments were important to the builders. But just how important were they? And how careful and how accurate were the builders when it came to astronomical alignment?

For scholars of the present generation, new research into these questions has led to lively and sometimes acerbic debate. It has been proposed (as we shall see in Chapter 5) that the builders and users of Stonehenge had developed astronomical and mathematical expertise far, far beyond their time and that the monument itself is a celestial observatory of extraordinary precision.

But scholars of Stukeley's day, and for a long time afterwards, were much less willing to credit the simple farmers of the megalithic era with the brain power necessary for such pursuits. They found other explanations. Stukeley himself, in fact, maintained that the plans for Stonehenge and all similar monuments were brought to Western Europe by wise men of Egypt after the conquest of their country by the Persians in 525 B.C. He saw their designs as so many Ptahs, or winged serpents—a sort of mystic hieroglyph stamped on the soil of England to transmit the esoteric wisdom of the ancients.

We now know that the megaliths are too old to be credited to Egyptians. But Stukeley's explanation was no more fanciful than some that came along in much more recent times.

About 50 years ago a provincial English salesman, tramping the fields and studying the ancient ruins, came to the conclusion that underlying the straight Roman roads lie still straighter primeval paths. He suggested that these paths form an interlocking pattern that covers the land and joins all the sites of greatest holiness and antiquity. Devotees of this Old Straight Track school have deduced that this pattern actually retraces the pattern of deep telluric currents, the magnetic lines of force that underlie the earth's surface. The ability (long since lost to modern knowledge) to identify and tap those mighty subterranean currents could only have come from such ancient treasure houses of wisdom as the lost continent of Atlantis (or perhaps from godlike visitors from outer space, like those who left behind the memorial stone in the movie *2001*).

Such a theory holds that stone circles like Stonehenge, built at the convergence of many lines of force, were a kind of power station concentrating energy in enormous quantities. People capable of hooking onto that energy at suitable moments when the sun and moon were in optimum position could then have used it not only to receive and transmit mystic messages but to move material objects as well. Within that theory, the building of Stonehenge would of course have been a much simpler matter than anyone has supposed: the stones would simply have been attached to the right line of force, and at the word of command they would have levitated and flown through the air to their point of destination.

If the builders of the megaliths could use these currents to fly, it would also give rational explanation to the old Irish legend of the Druid Mog Ruith, who was flying a megalith over St. George's Channel but crashed and was killed. Perhaps, it is suggested, this ancient aviator was using an inadequate almanac and was caught short by an unexpected eclipse of the moon that abruptly cut off the current powering his flight. There are those sobersides who doubt the whole story, but the very stone was set up by Mog Ruith's daughter near Tipperary, where it can be seen by doubters to this day.

Little is known for sure about the Druids. They were the priesthood of the Celtic warrior aristocracy that spread over Western Europe centuries after the megaliths were built. But popular imagination has long connected them with ancient sites of all sorts, and the megaliths are no exception. The 19th Century French Romantic Chateaubriand has left a vivid —though of course imagined—description of the beautiful blonde Druidess Velléda conducting a human sacrifice among the dark stones of Carnac:

"The crowd demands with a great cry the sacrifice of a human victim, in order to better learn the will of heaven. . . . The Druidess was obliged to declare that, since there was no designated victim, religion demanded an old man as the sacrifice most agreeable to Teutatès. Immediately an iron basin was brought, over which Velléda could cut the throat of the old man. They placed the basin on the ground before her. She was seated on a bronze tripod, her clothes in disarray, her hair wild, a poniard in her hand, a torch flaming at her feet. . . . The bards sang on: 'Teutatès wants blood. . . . The holy mistletoe has been cut with the golden sickle. . . . Teutatès wants blood, he has spoken in the oak of the Druids.' "

The 20th Century English romantic Robert Graves has abandoned the Druids in the light of more recent archaeological research, but the taste for blood remains in his poetic imagery nevertheless. Graves sees the stone circles as the scene of a yearly ritual in which the sacred king of the Waxing Year, who has ruled over the tribe for six months, is doubled over backwards and tied with a fivefold bond to an oak stump. He is surrounded by a circle of howling moon priestesses who are stoned to a frenzy on hallucinogenic mushrooms. The priestesses chant "Kill! Kill! Kill!" as they close in on him in an orgiastic dance that ends only after they castrate him, flay him, hack off his limbs and scatter his blood to fructify themselves and their mother, the earth.

The factual material that would substantiate such visions is slight. A split skull of a three-year-old child was found at Woodhenge, and the bones of a dwarf discovered at Windmill Hill near Avebury; these may have been victims offered at the inauguration of the monuments. But nothing else in the archaeological records indicates that any of the great structures was ever used for ritual slayings.

Observers throughout the ages have come up with many (more or less fanciful) theories of a nonspiritual nature to account for the erection of the megaliths. In the 17th Century Dr. Walter Charleton, Physician-in-Ordinary to King Charles II, gave it as his opinion that Stonehenge was a polling booth, built by the Danes when they ruled the land, for use at the election and inauguration of their kings. He wrote: "Plain stones laid overthwart upon the Tops of the Columns [were for a] convenient and firm footing for such persons of honourable condition who were principally to give their votes at the election of the King."

As wry John Aubrey remarked, "Tis a monstrous height for the grandees to stand: they had need to be very sober, and have good Heads: not vertiginous."

A French scholar of Revolutionary days announced that the stones of Carnac had been set up by Julius Caesar to provide firm supports for the tents of his army in that windy country.

Her eyes turned heavenwards and her breast bared, a Druid priestess presides over a human sacrifice at Carnac in a scene imagined by the 19th Century French artist Viollet-le-Duc. Although Viollet-le-Duc and many of his contemporaries assumed that such rites were standard practice in the age of the megaliths, nothing like them had actually occurred.

More recent students have started from the premise that if Stonehenge and the other megalithic monuments are temples, they are the only temples in the world with no dwelling places found near by. How could people living in flimsy tents and wooden huts have palaces built around an interior court and inhabited by warrior aristocrats like the Greek heroes of the *Iliad*? They certainly do not *look* anything like palaces, and it is difficult to see how kings could have held court in them without having left some traces of their presence.

As is always the case with archaeology, the lack of any eyewitness evidence makes a sure explanation impossible. Such an eyewitness would undoubtedly have things to report that could not be imagined by later students simply viewing the physical site. For example, an anthropologist in the Australian desert not long ago found a valley containing 436 roughly aligned stones, some 40 of them still upright. They were not of a size to count as megaliths but were imposing enough in that desolate land. He might have lost himself forever in speculations on their meaning, but fortunately an aborigine of a tribe that comes yearly to tend those stones could explain what they were. They were not the record of an event, he said, they *were* the event itself—the circumcision of an ancestor of the tribe in the far-off past known as the dream time. One of the stones stained with red streaks is his bleeding penis, and the other 435 are ancestral figures of totemic marsupial cat people who are assisting at the initiation.

For all we know, the stones at Stonehenge also may have exotic totemistic connotations that we cannot even begin to guess. They may have had many meanings over the centuries in which they were put up. In fact, almost the only explanation that has never been offered is that they had no meaning at all but were put up just for fun.

Still, it is difficult not to conclude that these stones, which were erected with such effort, were intended for a purpose that we would describe as religious, that they were designed to stamp the whole country, in Stukeley's words, "with the impress of a sacred character". The peasant population of Europe, despite all the repeated waves of conquest, is still partly neolithic in blood and still cherishes ancient practices and superstitions and perhaps even some traces of language that go back to neolithic times. The peasants who live near any great megalith almost always regard it with reverence and a certain fear. Early church councils were continually issuing decrees forbidding "oaths by sun and moon . . . offerings to stones and trees, leaps and dances over fires". It is clear that they were fighting to suppress ancient and tenacious beliefs that persisted long after the official religion had been changed.

If the megaliths are religious monuments, at least in part, who or what was the deity invoked in the ceremonies held at Stonehenge? Did the god or gods have a name? If so, we will never know it (though Robert Graves claims to have worked it out from old Welsh verses in *The White Goddess*: JIEVOAO).

It is possible, however, that if the deity took a personal form, that form was originally female. All the religious myths and rituals of pre-Christian Europe contain hints and traces of an older cult dedicated to a mother goddess, creator and destroyer of life, whose functions and privileges were in later religions usurped by male gods.

Text continued on page 61

Strange Theories about a Puzzling Monument

INIGO JONES.

STUKELY.

WOOD.

SMITH.

Hardly had the Norman invaders conquered England in 1066 when antiquarians began to puzzle over the whys and wherefores of the lonely megaliths of Stonehenge. Counting the monument among the wonders of Britain, one writer ventured cautiously in 1130 that no one could "guess by what means so many stones were raised so high, or why they were built there". Only six years later, a more imaginative chronicler, Geoffrey of Monmouth, posed what seemed to him a perfectly rational explanation: the omniscient necromancer Merlin had employed magic to import Stonehenge from Ireland.

Geoffrey's wisdom was unquestioningly accepted for nearly 500 years —until in the 17th Century the fertile minds of more scientifically inclined speculators began germinating more plausible explanations.

By the turn of the 20th Century, Stonehengeology had become such a popular pursuit that a bibliography of theories was compiled—including 947 entries. Some of the diverse notions are represented on these pages.

Representative of the unending fascination with Stonehenge, a page from a book by Sir Richard Colt Hoare, a renowned British antiquarian of the 19th Century, shows an artist's reconstruction of how the megaliths supposedly looked at the time they were erected. The four ground plans are interpretations of the puzzling monument by artists of other eras.

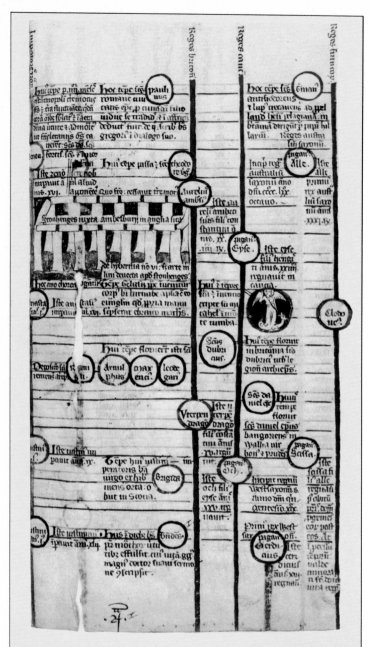

Colonnades of megaliths forming a rectangle (upper left) represent the oldest known depiction of Stonehenge on a page from a 14th Century manuscript. This manuscript recounts a theory first posed 200 years earlier by Geoffrey of Monmouth, that in 483 a Briton king named Aurelius Ambrosius sought to commemorate warriors fallen in a decisive battle against the Saxons. The king consulted the magician Merlin, who advised that he "send for the Giants' Dance which is in Killaraus, a mountain in Ireland. . . . They are stones of vast size and a wonderful quality, and if they can be brought here they will stand forever." Merlin lent a hand in moving the stones—and indeed they stood forever.

Jumbled, unhewn boulders standing in a circle like figures frozen in a frenzy of motion illustrate a theory that was current until the mid-1600s: that the megaliths were remnants of giants who, for some unknown reason, turned to stone while dancing. This notion was reviewed in 1663 by Dr. Walter Charleton, a physician to King Charles II, who undertook to refute all previous theories about Stonehenge. In a tome ponderously entitled "Chorea Gigantum: or, the Most Famous Antiquity of Great Britain, Vulgarly called Stone-heng, Standing on Salisbury-Plain, Restored to the Danes," Charleton put forth his own interpretation of the monument: the Danes built it (far right).

1. *The Trench.*
2. *The Entrance thereat from the North-East.*
3. *The two Pyramids thereof, on the outside of the Trench.*
4. *The other two on the inside.*
5. *The Pylasters of the outward Circle, or Supporters of the open Gallery, as G. Cambrensis hath it.*
6. *The Architraves incumbent on them.*
7. *The Perpendicular Stones of the Inner Circle.*
8. *The Pylasters of the Greater Hexagon.*
9. *The Architraves that adorn them.*
10. *The Pylasters of the Lesser Hexagon.*

Classical symmetry characterizes the reconstruction of
Stonehenge by Inigo Jones, the 17th Century architect who
declared that the Romans "only amongst all the nations of
the universe" could have created such a wonder.
Accordingly, Jones declared the monument a temple that
conformed to Tuscan architectural principles, erected by the
Romans and dedicated to an obscure God, Coelus. Jones
based his theory on readings in the classics and on first-hand
research among the ruins in France and Italy. The
monument's uprights were close together because, he said
one rule of Roman architecture dictated that "the greater
the columns were, the closer they set them together".

A. *The Kongstolen broad, flat, and of a Circular Form.*
B. *The stones wedged under it, and lying in round about it; upon
which for their greater security, and more reverend addresses
to the King, the Electors stood, not much higher than the surface
of the Earth, as common reason, without having recourse to
any Drawing, or other Authority must grant.*
C. *The King Elected.*
D. *The Electors.*
E. *The People.*
The Interpretation of the Inscription our Author affords us not.

Behold Doctor *Charletons Stone-Heng.*

A Danish polling place for electing and inaugurating kings
was the theory advanced by Dr. Walter Charleton. Dating
Stonehenge's construction back to a time when Denmark
ruled Britain, Charleton claimed that "the ancient courts of
parliament in Denmark always were situated in large and
open plains . . . near to the middle of the kingdom".
Charleton described a structure exactly like Stonehenge
—although his drawing hardly resembled it—where a king
would stand on top of the highest stone so "that the common
people, assembled to confirm the suffrage of the electors, by
their universal applause and congratulatory acclamations,
might see and witness the solemn manner of the election".

Stukeley. d.

Worshipful Druids lurk among hulking megaliths in a drawing by the 18th Century antiquarian William Stukeley, who pronounced Stonehenge a Druid temple. The Druids, according to Stukeley, were a sect of Phoenician priests who came to Britain during the time of Abraham. Their homeland, he alleged, was Canaan, the same as Abraham's; and their religion venerated the same God as the Christians'. In this circuitous fashion Stukeley construed the Druids as suitable ancestors for pious 18th Century Englishmen and their temple a fitting precursor of English cathedrals.

This mother goddess is found in thousands of images all over the ancient world, from the fat, lumpy figurines of Cro-Magnon times to the lithe, wasp-waisted statues on Crete. Certain stylized representations of the female figure, resembling what are regarded as female symbols in the eastern Mediterranean, can be found in megalithic sites in the north of Europe. Round circles, which may stand for the goddess' eyes, and protuberances, which may represent her breasts, are standard features on the walls of decorated megalithic tombs and on occasional menhirs. It has been suggested that the odd bulbous ground plans of the temples of Malta were traced to represent the goddess as a fat, pregnant woman, the source of all fecundity.

That snakes should also be carved on her shrines is not surprising, for she was Mother Earth. Snakes lived in her bosom, and in ancient times snakes were used as oracles for imparting the goddess' secrets into the ears of priestesses. It was not until much later, as explained in Genesis, that an angry male deity decreed unending war between woman and serpent.

In the 44th chapter of Jeremiah, the prophet tells how he went to Pathros in Egypt after the destruction of Jerusalem by Nebuchadnezzar and found an angry clump of Jewish refugees there. They upbraided him for his loyalty to what they regarded as a usurping male sky god, Jehovah, whom they blamed for all their calamities. Defiantly they told him they would go back to the good old ways and "burn incense unto the queen of heaven and pour out drink offerings unto her, as we have done, we and our fathers, our kings and our princes, in the cities of Judah, and in the streets of Jerusalem: for then had we plenty of victuals, and were well, and saw no evil".

Surely Queen of Heaven must have been one of the titles by which the first joyful celebrants of Salisbury Plain greeted their goddess when she brought up the sun—the source of food and health and prosperity—to dance on the Heel Stone of Stonehenge.

Chapter Three: Settlers and Builders

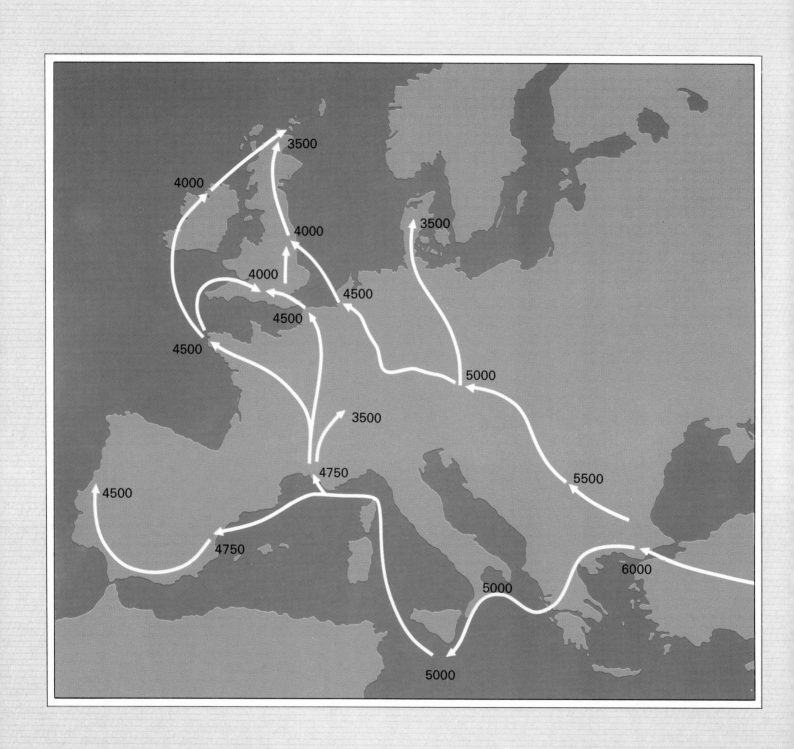

Who were these builders of mammoth megaliths? Where did they come from and how did they develop a society that produced such an extraordinary monumental heritage? Their ancestors were mainly farmers—neolithic people who began to filter into Europe from the Middle East shortly before 6000 B.C. These immigrants approached Europe by two main routes. Some of them sailed westwards along the northern shores of the Mediterranean—presumably in dugouts or possibly in skin-covered boats—settling mostly on islands and in coastal areas. Others crossed the Aegean into Greece and the Balkans and slowly pushed inland and northwards through mountain passes and up the valley of the Danube. Within the relatively brief span of 1,500 years, descendants of these pioneer groups had spread their agricultural villages across much of the continent and had developed a stable way of life that allowed ample time for the building of enduring monuments in stone.

The farmers whose ancestors came up through the Balkans settled as far north and west as the Low Countries and adjoining parts of France. The descendants of the farmers who had come along the Mediterranean coast made their way to Spain and Portugal, followed the Rhone Valley to northwestern France and by about 4000 B.C. crossed the Channel to Britain and Ireland. It was among these farming communities of Western and temperate northern Europe that megalith building developed about 4500 B.C.—and it was among them that it lasted longest.

What prompted the Middle East farmers to migrate to Europe can only be conjectured. There is good reason to believe that population pressure, coupled with the limited amount of food that could be produced by still-primitive farming methods, may have been the significant reasons. Archaeology has shown that since the Neolithic Revolution—the birth of farming in the Middle East around 9000 B.C.—agricultural villages in that part of the world grew in size as well as in number, and in many of them the population must have increased to the point where there were more people than could be supported by the community's fields and herds. The solution in such cases would have been for some families to emigrate, taking with them their wheat, barley and other cultivated plants and their domesticated animals. It was probably in this way, by moving away from an overpopulated parent village every few generations, that by about 6000 B.C. groups of farmers eventually reached the threshold of Europe—the eastern shores of the Mediterranean and the Aegean.

The continent into which these settlers ventured was geographically and climatically much like the Europe of today. In a few places the coastline has risen or sunk since then and some lakes have spread or contracted. But the mountains and plains and rivers that the settlers saw were virtually the same. At the time of their arrival the warming of the climate after the retreating glaciers of the last ice age was essentially completed. By 5000 B.C. their descendants would know a climate so like that of the present that if a modern European were transported back some 7,000 years he would hardly notice the difference.

Seeking new land for their expanding numbers, the farming forebears of Europe's monument builders crossed the Bosporus about 6000 B.C. and made their way westwards and northwards across Europe, as indicated by the arrows on map at left. The settlers moved more than 20 miles every generation. Some travelled by boat along the Mediterranean coast, others walked the meandering river valleys. After about 3,000 years the journey ended in the north of Scotland.

Only the landscape of temperate Europe has altered beyond recognition since the time of the early farmers. The orderly countryside of today was then a wilderness of almost continuous deciduous forest, so that the clearings the arriving farmers made for their early settlements were surrounded by dense green stands of trees, like islands in a gigantic, leafy sea. It must have taken courage, besides the pressure of a growing population, for succeeding generations to move forward into that dark, damp and unknown land. The snow and ice that imprisoned the settlers during the winter, the dank marshes, the immense distances all conspired with the forest to shut off communities from each other. Passage from village to village meant river travel or the clearing of miles of pathways along the drier upland ridges where the forest grew more sparsely. And even where the forest was less dense, its perils—real or imaginary —might lurk behind any mossy tree trunk: wolves and lynxes, adders, hostile woodland spirits and the hulking, powerful bear, whom man had contested for the possession of caves since the ice age.

But the forest that held such terrors and mysteries —as it still does in European fairy tales—at the same time provided an inexhaustible storehouse of food, fuel and raw materials for those who learned to live in it. With its timbers the farmers could build solid houses and warm themselves all winter with roaring fires. The soil of the clearings they had hacked out with stones axes was made fertile by decayed vegetation and further enriched by the ashes of burning-off. It produced heavy crops, even if only for a few years at a time. Without regular manuring, the over-worked soil gradually became exhausted; but usually there was more virgin forest land farther on to be

Three finely polished axe blades, dating from about 1800 B.C., *show the precision and artistry with which stone tools were fashioned by neolithic men in Britain. Cut from easily flaked rock such as flint or basalt, the blades were often shaped to simulate the metal implements ushered in by the Copper Age.*

cleared and planted afresh. Among the trees around the fringes of the clearings the farmer's cattle, sheep and goats could find sufficient grazing, and his pigs could fatten themselves on fallen nuts and acorns.

If his crops failed occasionally and wolves killed off his stock, he did not always starve; at such times he could turn to hunting the deer, wild boar, wild cattle and smaller game that abounded in the forest. The rivers teemed with fish. If his forest settlement was near the sea, the newcomer could forage on shores that were sometimes almost solid banks of oysters. Nature's bounty on such a scale would not be seen again by Europeans until thousands of years later, when descendants of the early farmers landed in North America to plunge into the green vistas that seemed to stretch forever westward.

Until the arrival of the first farmers, all the inhabitants of Europe had been hunter-gatherers, entirely dependent on what nature provided. About 800,000 years ago recognizable humans (Homo erectus) were becoming established in Europe. Early in the last ice age Europe's lowlands sometimes became as cold as present-day Lapland, and most of the landscape was treeless tundra covered with low-growing shrubs, mosses and grasses. In this forbidding landscape Neanderthals hunted woolly mammoths. Later in the ice age came more modern men, the well-organized Cro-Magnon hunters who were armed with superbly made stone-pointed spears; their principal prey were the reindeer, bison and other big game that abounded in enormous herds on the grass-steppe tundra of Western and central Europe.

Around 15,000 to 12,000 B.C., the ice sheets gradually melted, leaving the landscape strewn with their debris, including huge boulders that in some parts of Europe would become a major raw material for construction of megaliths. Slowly the climate of much of Europe grew less rigorous, and the cold-loving tundra vegetation was replaced at first by scrub, then birch, then pine forest and finally by the deciduous forest of oak, ash and elm that ultimately reached as far north as what is now south-central Sweden. Meanwhile, the reindeer and other big-game animals hunted by Cro-Magnon men had moved ahead of the northward-advancing forest to regions where cooler conditions still prevailed. Some groups of people followed the reindeer farther and farther north and continued to live mainly by big-game hunting, but others remained in more southerly parts of Europe and learned to cope with the slowly changing environment. They had to satisfy themselves with hunting forest animals such as red deer; and since the forest provided more wild plants than the ice age tundras, they probably gathered vegetable foods more intensively than their predecessors.

The 3,000 or so years that preceded the introduction of farming into Western Europe is known as the Mesolithic, or Middle Stone, Age. During this era hunter-gatherers not only adjusted rapidly and successfully to environmental change but they also made considerable technological progress. In mesolithic times a number of important innovations appeared in Europe, among them dugout canoes, fish traps and the bow and arrow, a more efficient hunting weapon than the stone- or antler-tipped spear.

It was bands of these mesolithic hunter-gatherers, then, that the ancestors of the megalith builders encountered as they gradually spread their farming communities through temperate Europe. There is no indication of serious conflict between the two groups. The earliest farmers did not defend their villages with palisades or ramparts, and in the remains of many villages mesolithic stone tools and neolithic artifacts have been found together, suggesting that in some areas newcomers and native people mingled freely.

The earliest farmers who entered Europe from the Middle East were probably all of the same racial stock, with roughly the same cultural traditions. But from the very beginning differences in form and quality began to distinguish the farming settlements of Europeans from those of the Middle Easterners. And, not surprisingly, these differences grew as succeeding generations of farmers moved westwards and northwards into Europe, away from the Middle East.

Meeting and sometimes mingling with the mesolithic hunter-gatherers probably altered the early farmers' life style in some decisive ways. The admixture of cultures, together with a cooler, wetter climate and a new set of resources for building, may have led to the major differences between the farmers of Europe and their Middle East counterparts: their houses and settlements. In western Asia, villages tended to be tight huddles of buildings made of dried packed mud or clay brick, the whole forming compact, mazelike structures well adapted for defence and for fostering tight communal ties. In thinly inhabited Europe, on the other hand, the nearest enemy was probably a long way off, and villages were groups of detached houses. Moreover, even the earliest of these were built not of mud alone, which would have deteriorated under the rains of temperate Europe, but of mud on a framework of stout timber posts. And as the settlers moved northwards, mud was used less,

and timber became the chief building material. From the start, changes in organization of the village itself must have been accompanied by changes in social structure; whereas the farming communities of the Middle East continued to be close-knit and hierarchical and eventually became urban, those of Europe remained small and more loosely connected, possibly reflecting a more egalitarian, less tightly organized society that may have been more inclined to join in large building projects.

But if their contact with Europe changed the farmers, so too did the farmers change the face of the land. As they spread by clearing the forest within easy reach of their settlements and moved on when the soil's fertility was exhausted, the natural environment underwent a gradual transformation; in some areas this was to prove nearly disastrous.

In northern Europe this transformation was relatively slight. The farmers found a seemingly inexhaustible supply of land. Once it became worked out, it could be left fallow for 20 years or so, a new tree cover could grow on it and refurnish it with critical nutrients, and the farmers could return to begin the slash-and-burn cycle of clearing over again.

In the south of Europe, in the more broken, drier countrysides bordering the Mediterranean, it was harder to get an assured living from the soil. After land had been cleared for fields, the alternation of drought and flash floods scarred the hillsides with rocky gullies, the topsoil was washed out of the valley floors, and eventually the forests of towering trees were gone. Nothing was left but tangles of scrub on stony soil, the maquis that still covers much of southern Europe. Towards the end of the megalith-building period, after 2000 B.C., deforestation and thinning of the soil, compounded by destructive overgrazing, had brought severe restrictions to both agriculture and the quality of human life in southern Europe.

At first, though, the problem was not to find cultivable land, for that existed in abundance, but to find land where the forest was thinner and more easily cleared and where lighter, better-drained soil made it especially favourable for agriculture. By combining the archaeological discoveries at various early megalithic sites in Europe with inferences drawn from them, it is possible to draw a representative portrait of these peoples who settled in Western Europe and who would cover it with megaliths.

A typical group of early settlers—perhaps fifty individuals with their livestock—would first move into a territory well suited to their needs. The trees in the area the settlers have chosen are more widely spaced than in most parts of the forest, and there is less undergrowth. But there is still much backbreaking work to be done before the land is sufficiently cleared for houses and crops.

At this stage there is neither sufficient time nor manpower to construct monuments, or even substantial homes. The women and older children put up temporary shelters—skin tents or brush huts—to keep off the rains of early summer. The men meanwhile start the clearing process. First they use their stone axes to cut a ring of bark from around the trees; this restricts the upward flow of sap and causes the trees to dry up and die. Later in the summer the men clear the undergrowth and set fire to the piles of cut vegetation. The fire, watchfully tended, reduces the undergrowth to ashes and meanwhile begins to eat at the drying and dying trees. Finally a tract of once-

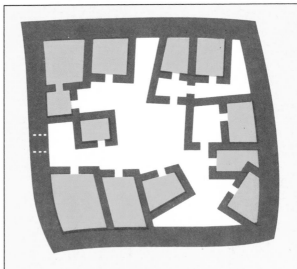

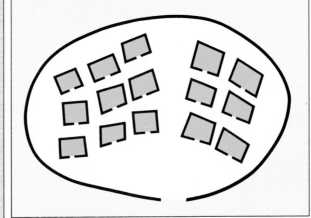

The typical early neolithic European community differed markedly from its Middle Eastern counterpart, as these village plans show. The average Middle Eastern village (above) grew completely within massive walls, needed for protection from raiders; its mudbrick houses were built at random with common supporting walls. In less crowded Europe a new village would be made up of individual timber and mud houses. Such a pioneer settlement might be encircled only by a flimsy cattle stockade.

green forest lies smoking and black, open to the sky.

In the meantime, the livestock, watched over by the older children, have had to make out largely on their own—the cattle and a few sheep and goats grazing on the lower branches of the trees around the clearing and on whatever scanty herbs and grasses they can find in the small forest glades, the swine grubbing for roots and acorns.

Depending upon their animals and some of the small supply of wheat and barley that they have brought with them from their earlier village, supplemented by the wild food resources of their new home, the group is able to survive through the autumn and winter. And during this time they start construction of a new village that will have enough proper houses to accommodate all the families. Their work is interrupted by the need to sow new crops of wheat and barley so the seeds will be ready to sprout with the coming of spring. The autumn rains have partly washed the ash into the ground and enriched it. The seeds can be easily planted by the women, who scrape hollows in the soil with sharp-pointed digging sticks and cover them with a cut branch to protect them from foraging creatures. The settlers can now look forward to a few years of rich harvest until the soil's fertility is depleted.

Only after the grain plots are prepared and planted can the settlers concentrate on completing their permanent houses. From the forest's unlimited supply of timber, the men cut stout posts. They stand these upright in holes dug in the ground, forming the framework of the walls for each house. The roof beams come next, followed by the pitched roof itself, covered with thatch or turf, protection against Europe's long, damp winters. The walls are then completed by binding the posts together with intertwined small boughs and by filling any remaining chinks with mud; this final touch is a job that finds willing helpers in the children who, then as now, find special delight in mud. Part of a finished house will be set aside for sheltering the livestock in wintertime and for storing the grain crop expected the following summer.

Finally, sheltered in permanent houses and with their first few seasons' crops gathered, the settlers have time to attend to other matters. Now their thoughts turn to the social and ceremonial life that sustains the community, cementing its relationships within itself and with both preceding and succeeding generations. And as with many other neolithic Europeans, this activity centres on the construction of a monument. This one will serve a double purpose. Two elderly members of the new village group have already died; they must be buried. A monument can provide for their burial and also serve as a centre for the community's ceremonial gatherings.

A level site is selected not far from the new village, and after the men have cleared it of trees and undergrowth they search the neighbourhood for rocks with which to build a worthy community tomb. Large surface boulders have been left by long-receded glaciers, and smaller ones litter a near-by river bed. Even the smallest of these boulders is far too heavy to be carried, and wheeled vehicles are unknown to these Europeans of about 4000 B.C., so the stones must be dragged to the tomb site on rough sledges, pulled by the men themselves or perhaps by the more tractable of their cattle. The sledges with the largest, heaviest boulders are slowly eased forward, inch by painful inch, on massive log rollers.

When completed, the tomb will be a gallery grave:

a low, narrow corridor some 30 feet long, its walls of close-set boulders supporting a roof made of several huge capstones weighing up to seven tons each. The whole will then be covered with a mound of earth, and when the remains of the recent dead are placed within it the entrance to the gallery grave will be covered with a flat rock that can be removed later for new burials. For these people dependent entirely on muscle power, the amount of labour expended on the tomb is immense, but there is satisfaction in knowing that their monument will serve generation after generation as a burial place and ceremonial centre.

A megalithic community, once settled in and prospering, must have been a fairly stable and conservative institution. Over many generations its life probably followed the same yearly round of planting and harvesting, of births and marriages and deaths, of ceremonial observances—a time-tested pattern that had proved practical and beneficial to the people and so persisted with little change.

But even such tradition-bound communities as these seemed willing to leave their monuments behind, if necessary, and move on to other areas, where they may have built other monuments. When the time came for a group to split off from or occasionally abandon the parent village—because it had used up the fertility of the soil, or grown too large for its territory or because feuds and rivalries had broken out between different families—its members were ready to venture into new and unknown regions.

It was this continuing willingness to risk the unknown that, between 4000 and 3500 B.C., led megalith builders to brave the uncharted waters of the English Channel and found their first settlements in Britain. It would, of course, have been folly for everyone to pack up and move off all at once. No doubt a scouting party of a dozen able-bodied men would make the initial crossing, probably in dugout canoes patterned after those used by their fishermen neighbours. After setting up a camp on the British coast and perhaps burning down some forest for future fields, the scouts would return with a favourable report, then sail back with new provisions. This time the advance party would spend a season in the new land, perhaps plant the first crops, build livestock enclosures and in general lay the foundation for a permanent settlement. There might have been many such preliminary trips and months of consolidation before the community met in council to decide on the fateful step of moving. Eventually, however, everybody and everything would be packed into boats —men, women and children, livestock, seed grain, axes, pots, baskets, sacred objects—ready to push out into the surf at the first sign of favourable weather.

Even in the best weather the crossing in such primitive craft would have been chancy, and the neolithic voyagers needed plenty of ingenuity, prayer and luck, combined with long and careful observation of winds and tides. No doubt many of them never made it. Besides dugout canoes, which would carry very little cargo, they may have had roomier boats made of ox-hides stretched over a light framework of wood. The modern Eskimos make crafts of this kind, called umiaks, using walrus or seal skins; they are watertight, weigh little and are easy to repair. Carvings in a passage grave in Brittany portray several vessels with high curves at bow and stern that perhaps represent umiak-like boats. British archaeologist Humphrey Case, an authority on prehistoric craft, estimates that vessels of this type, about 30 feet long, could be handled by eight men or women rowing or paddling and one steersman. They could carry a total weight of three tons of cargo, crew and passengers. Their load for the Channel crossing might have been two cows and two calves, or six pigs, or 10 sheep and goats.

These boats may have been transformed into crude sailing craft by lashing amidships a mast made of an upright sapling, complete with leafy branches to catch the breeze; animal hide would be too heavy for a sail. The boats so equipped could sail only before the wind. More likely the small ships were powered by paddles, but however they were propelled, a single high sea breaking over these deckless boats could ruin the voyagers' supplies of seed grain and leave them to face a desperate winter. With a favourable wind it might be an easy passage, but the seas around Britain are notoriously unpredictable and normally choppy; and if the weather turned bad it might take days to get across the Channel. Meanwhile, there would be all the passengers and animals to be kept calm and fed. The pigs and even the cows might be tractable. But a nervous bull, even though tied and blindfolded to lessen his terror, might rip the delicate shell of the boat and drown everyone.

All neolithic peoples who eventually settled beyond the confines of continental Europe had to face such problems; yet they seem to have taken them all easily in their stride. They made sea voyages not just to Britain but to the Orkneys and the Shetlands farther north, and across still wilder waters to Ireland in the west. With the possible exception of some Bronze Age traders who may have crossed the North Sea, not until the time of the Vikings in the Early Middle Ages did Europeans begin to show the boldness

and the knowledgeable confidence that would permit them to brave sailing out into the North Sea and the Atlantic in open boats.

Travelling by water and land, between 6000 and 3500 B.C., neolithic settlers established themselves across most of Europe and spread to many outlying islands. Where one group came from, by just what route it got to its new home, how it interacted with its neighbours are questions still argued by specialists. They identify groups of neolithic Europeans by pottery shards or tools—for example, the axes and corded pottery of the Battle-Axe People who seem to have moved through Europe in the Third Millennium. But only rarely can such finds be clearly interpreted.

This uncertainty stems from the fact that neolithic Europeans seem to have shared a similar culture. Probably they defended their homes against intruders, but there were no national boundaries as we know them to keep techniques or ideas from spreading fairly rapidly over the continent. The differences between neolithic Europeans were often regional; some more southerly peoples are thought to have been mainly agricultural; others farther north may have concentrated on stock raising.

In only one case is there solid evidence that an alien people may have moved in with the existing neolithic population, adding elements of their own to its basically homogeneous culture. These were the Beaker People, so called because they used and frequently buried abstractly decorated beakers—bell-shaped, reddish-brown pottery drinking cups—in the megalithic tombs of their dead. They seem to have arrived in Western Europe sometime in the Third Millennium B.C. in successive waves, scattering their

the quality of life during those three long millennia.

Life on the whole was undoubtedly simple. Spellbound by spectacular feats like moving 300-ton boulders or the accomplishment of packing cattle into frail skin-covered boats to cross miles of unknown water, prehistorians have tended to overemphasize the strains and labours of megalithic man. He was indeed capable of spurts and starts of enormous physical energy, and he could work for extended periods of time if he needed to, inching the giant boulders along miles of country. But there is no reason to think that he spent all or even a majority of his time on such projects. He was in many ways a man of leisure. The climate was salubrious, the land was fertile. The hardy herds of cattle and swine more or less took care of themselves. If crops occasionally failed, wild game was always within reach, and edible herds and berries grew wild in the forest clearings. If a house burned down, a new one could be put up with the aid of friendly neighbours.

Such an existence does not jibe with the commonly held conception of prehistoric people forever struggling with nature in order to survive. Far from being exhausted by the struggle with nature, the megalith builders seem to have achieved a remarkably happy balance with their surroundings. They were apparently a healthy, moderately prosperous and generally peaceful people, earning their living from the soil without too much strain and with ample time left over for constructing monuments and taking part in ceremonies around them. They were open to innovation but faithful to tradition, maintaining a stable way of life for some 3,000 years, with a slowly increasing standard of living but no abrupt revolutionary changes until the introduction of metal.

Perhaps it was not quite as rosy as all that. But as man moved forward into the bright and often cruel light of history, there remained in the recesses of his mind, for a while at least, a vague recollection of a time when he lived more at harmony with his environment than he ever would again.

The poet Hesiod, writing on mainland Greece in the Eighth Century B.C., hundreds of years after the final megalith had been built in Europe, could look around and see little but woe—overworked soils, deforested mountains, people crowded into unhealthy cities and slaughtering each other wholesale over parcels of land and handfuls of barren metal. Nature's bounty could only be reaped by year-long drudgery, and man's hand was raised everywhere against his brother. The degenerate present of Hesiod's day contrasted vividly in the poet's mind with legends that had come down to him of a past when men had enjoyed a life that was open and easy and peaceful. He called it the Golden Age:

They lived as if they were gods,
Their hearts free from all sorrow . . .
When they died, it was as if they fell asleep . . .

The fruitful grainland yielded its harvest to them
*   of its own accord . . .*
while they at their pleasure
quietly looked after their works,
in the midst of good things . . .

While Hesiod may have been seeing the past through a golden haze, his vision may well have contained elements of prosaic fact. Perhaps in the long course of history, megalithic times were indeed man's closest approach to a golden age.

Pioneers in a New Land

The ancestors of the mighty megalith builders of France and England were stolid farming folks well acquainted with the rigours of converting forests into farmland. Over the course of 2,500 years they had migrated in a slow, steady stream from the Middle East across Europe, eternally driven by the need for new, fresh soil.

The industrious group of farmers at left has successfully survived the first year in a new settlement cleared out of the forest in northern France. They have cut down a section of oak and elm to make room for grazing land and a small garden, and have built a house large enough to shelter about 25 people. After erecting the structure's vertical sides, they plugged the cracks with mud and straw. The chimneyless roof is thatched with some reeds from a near-by river.

In the background the settlers are preparing more farmland; earlier they had stripped the bark off the bases of the trees, and now they are setting the dry trunks afire. In the foreground, three of the women sow vegetable seeds in the rich soil.

The soil will not always be so fruitful. However, ashes from the burned trees will fertilize it for many seasons, but then the land will become exhausted. The farmers will be forced to follow their centuries-old pattern of moving on to yet another settlement, perhaps even in another land.

Across the Water to Found Another Colony

The farmers of megalithic Europe—a venturesome and hardy breed—would clear one patch of wilderness, cultivate it, then move on across the continent. Some eventually reached the English Channel, and a few intrepid spirits decided to risk its waters and settle the land on the other side. They probably sent scouts ahead to explore the terrain, to hack out clearings and, of most immediate importance, to find the narrowest part of the Channel. These investigations completed, the voyagers could make preparations to depart.

In the artist's conception at right, the people are warmly clad in clothes made of animal hides. Into one of the skin boats at the edge of the shore women load provisions, while in the other men clear a place amidships for weapons, tools and animals. All these supplies have been hauled to the site on a heavy wooden sledge (*centre right*) lashed together with ropes made of plant fibres. In the foreground one man places a hide covering over a clay container filled with seeds to protect them from the salt spray that would destroy them, while other men truss goats and pigs to prevent horns and hoofs from piercing the boats' sides.

Finally, men, women, children and watchdogs will pile into the boats for the toughest challenge of all: navigating the treacherous currents of the Channel towards their new homeland.

In a Settled Community, Time for a Burial Ceremony

Once the megalithic farmers had settled into their communities, they had time to devote to ceremonial activities. One of these was tomb building for burials. The drawing of a burial ceremony at right is based on the findings at West Kennet Long Barrow, just south of Avebury, England.

A barrow was a multiroomed neolithic tomb that could accommodate at least 50 bodies. West Kennet Barrow was 330 feet long but only six feet above the ground. Its turf-covered dome is cut away in this artist's depiction in which a procession of mourners enters the barrow carrying three bodies for interment. Two other members of the party, bearing torches, inspect the innermost of the five chambers, already filled with skeletal remains and bodies more recently laid to rest. Of the three corpses being brought in, two are shrouded, indicating that they had been kept in an ossuary, or temporary burial place. West Kennet was opened only infrequently so that several dead might be interred in one collective ceremony.

A mystery still unsolved by archaeologists concerns the number of bones uncovered at West Kennet. Although about 50 bodies have been accounted for, they lack either skulls or long leg bones or both. Whether these parts were pulverized to make room for new arrivals or removed for some ritualistic purpose is unknown.

Chapter Four: The Evidence of the Tombs

The people who built the megaliths for all eternity built their own homes of perishable wood, mud and reeds. Since fire, rain and rot have removed most traces of these less durable structures, it is more difficult to find out about the places where neolithic men resided in earthly life than it is to learn about those they provided for the hereafter.

Still, some clues remain. Some have turned up in surprising discoveries of the remains of entire settlements; some come from scattered fragments. Others can be deduced by analogy to societies that today live at the neolithic level in such areas as New Guinea and the Trobriand Islands. Taken together, all these clues give a picture of human life in Europe between 4500 and 1500 B.C. It is a picture of men who farmed and fished and hunted, who manufactured stone tools and traded them far and wide. Evidently their society was egalitarian; certainly they held religious beliefs and engaged in rituals from time to time.

Of the many thousands of sites where neolithic man lived, only a few survive. One of the best examples is at Skara Brae, in the Orkney Islands off the northwest coast of Scotland, where a whole village of 10 houses was uncovered in 1850 by a storm from the sand that had drifted over it. When archaeologists completed nature's excavation in 1928, the village was found to have been untouched since 1500 B.C.; except for the roofs it was structurally in-

A necklace of amber and shale beads went with an Early Bronze Age woman to her grave in Upton Lovell, England. A hole had been painstakingly bored through each bead. Originally they were probably held together with sinew threaded through the beads with a bone needle, but the sinew has disintegrated; the necklace has been restrung.

tact. And the reason it survived in such near-pristine condition was that—like the megaliths that had been erected in the same era—it was built of stone. Its founders, who dared rough seas to reach this distant, desolate place and settled down to a rude life as herders and fishermen, found little timber on the island to build with. But the seashore was covered with shale, which makes an ideal construction material because it breaks off into long, thin, sturdy flakes. They used this flagstone to build houses in the shape of the wooden cabins they probably were accustomed to on the mainland.

All the houses at Skara Brae have stone walls 10 feet high. The roofs—now fallen to the floors—were made of whale jawbone, which probably supported hides. Outdoors, the walls of the houses were surrounded by the accumulated refuse of daily life —fish, animal bones and sea shells. This rubbish may have served as effective insulation against the fierce Atlantic gales and provided a snug, if smelly, interior. The remains of this debris gave the archaeologists who excavated Skara Brae ample evidence of the means by which the people sustained themselves—cattle and sheep herding, fishing, gathering shellfish along the rocky shores.

Indoors, each house has a central hearth, stone bedsteads and stone storage cubicles and shelves. On a shelf in one house the excavators found a pot still standing where the prehistoric housewife had put it. There are storage spaces dug into the stone floors and others built into the walls. There are drains under the floors. The houses were neat, efficiently designed and eminently practical, even by 20th Century standards. When the archaeologists were digging at the site, they hired a local woman to cook and clean; she moved into one of the prehistoric houses and lived there quite comfortably.

Another kind of evidence of neolithic life has turned up in the wind-swept bogland of north County Mayo, in the west of Ireland. Here the clues lie not in housing but in the land. The bog blankets thousands of square miles and is cut for fuel near present-day settlements. As the cutting reaches the base of the peat, usually five or six feet down, the land surface on which the peat originally formed is exposed, and an astonishing picture emerges. Archaeologists have found below the bog stumps of an ancient forest and a coherent field-division pattern. There is evidence, too, of sophisticated cultivation.

Scientists once dated the beginning of the bog at around 600 B.C., since that was when temperate Europe slowly turned from a warmer climate to the conditions that prevail today: fairly mild winters, cool summers and rainfall evenly distributed throughout the year. But undisturbed settlements have been found just below the bog, and pot shards in them have been dated as far back as 2000 B.C. In the absence of another layer between the remains and the bog, archaeologists conclude that the bog must have begun to form about 1500 B.C. Unlike most regions where prehistoric man lived, this area was never disturbed by later ploughing, despoiled by contractors in search of gravel or buried by cities. It lies just as it did when neolithic man last saw it.

Western Ireland thus offers a unique opportunity to explore the neolithic countryside—to find out what land was cultivated, grazed or left wooded; to discover the system used to divide one plot of land from another; to compare the relative size of not just a few but many adjacent settlements; to determine how many settlements and how many tombs lie in the same area. Here, at last, is the archaeologists' dream: the chance to examine a whole undisturbed neolithic landscape.

So far their work is at a very early stage, but excavation is going forward in at least four sites: Ballyglass, Carrownaglogh, Behy-Glenulra and Belderg. At Ballyglass the remains of a rectangular neolithic house have been found. At Carrownaglogh there is evidence of clearing and enclosed cultivation in neolithic times. At Behy-Glenulra, which is on a slope, the findings indicate that a large tract of land was divided by long parallel stone walls into enclosed fields that may have been individual farms; the living areas and cultivated plots were at the downhill end; the grazing areas were uphill. The dig at Belderg has been an eye opener for students of early farming methods. There, in a small farm that lay close to the edge of the ancient forest, the land at the neolithic level has been carefully ridged, indicating that the ground was spaded into hilly rows to make the most of the rather thin topsoil; until this discovery, ridging was not thought to have been practised until the Middle Ages. At the bottom of the cultivated soil, where it lies on paler subsoil, are faint but clear traces of plough furrows, running in two directions at right angles to each other, one direction parallel to the ridges. This is the largest and one of the earliest examples of prehistoric cross-ploughing found anywhere in Europe.

These sites, as the work on them proceeds, open up fascinating aspects of neolithic society. The field walls at Behy-Glenulra, which are parallel, form a pattern that indicates the laying out of land on a large, orderly scale, not unlike the geometric layout of the land-grant system used in the U.S. during the 19th Century settlement of the West. And whether or not such a system demonstrates the existence of centralization, it certainly demonstrates that neolithic man was a capable organizer.

Not the least of the tantalizing puzzles is the question of whether the County Mayo sites and Skara Brae are typical of the thousands of other settlements that dotted neolithic Europe. Such are the handicaps under which students of the period must labour: the physical remains are infinitesimal compared to what has been lost, and they may be exceptions or oddities rather than the rule. But the remains are all there to study, and, as the British archaeologist R. J. C. Atkinson, an expert on Stonehenge, says, "The raw material of prehistory is not men, but things." Out of these things, few and recalcitrant as they may be, scholars have provided at least a glimpse of what life may have been like in neolithic times. As the 17th Century scholar Sir Thomas Browne expressed it, the archaeologist's goal is "to preserve the living and to make the dead to live".

Sometimes finds of stray objects can be as revealing of megalithic life as entire settlements are. Some burial sites, for example, have yielded remains of a variety of musical instruments. In Bohemia (now part of Czechoslovakia) hourglass-shaped clay drums have been unearthed that produce resonant booms when uncured leather is stretched over them. The drums are of varying sizes, indicating that their inventors understood pitch as well as rhythm. In Ireland, England and Scandinavia excavators have found cow horns with holes in their sides that sound like trumpets. A Dublin physician named Dr. Robert Ball came to grief in 1860 while trying to prove that one of these cow horns was a genuine musical instrument. "It is a melancholy fact", the *Ulster Journal of Archaeology* reported that year, that "in the act of attempting to produce a distinct sound . . . he burst a blood vessel and died a few days later". More prudent palaeo-organologists (as students of prehistoric music call themselves) have safely played on a variety of primitive flutes, pipes and ocarinas and have produced musical sounds—though they cannot agree whether the instruments were designed to produce notes on a five-tone, an eight-tone or a no-tone scale. They must have played in one way or another, perhaps as an accompaniment to the work of megalith building; it is easy to imagine workers heaving their burdens to the insistent urging of pipes and the steady beat of drums. It is also plausible to surmise that the drums were used to send messages through the forest and over the hills.

Musical instruments, of course, are rare finds. Of all the surviving prehistoric objects, the most common are tools—because the durability of rock (of which most were made) has ensured their survival, and because they were so widespread. Uncounted numbers of hammers, axes, saws, awls, scrapers, chisels, knives, chippers and hoes exist. They attest to the variety and precision of the crafts of neolithic man and tell something of his economy as well.

Stone Age man had over tens of thousands of years in which to become increasingly skilled at making tools and weapons out of the random pieces of rock he found lying about on the ground. In pioneering conditions or on long hunting trips his very existence depended on this skill. In the course of time he learned that better tools could be made of outcrop-

Barbed arrowheads have been found in
Brittany and in England, where some
were unearthed in a barrow used for
the cremation of an archer. Made of
flint, they have finely tooled openings
for the insertion of wooden shafts that
have long since disintegrated. Their
lethal points and razor-sharp edges
were used for felling game, not men.

pings of rock found on the earth's surface, often flint or some other sharply splintering material. And he learned how to pry blocks loose and then flake or chip them down to the desired size and shape. As he worked his way deeper into the veins of flint, he discovered that the quality was more likely to improve the farther he got from the weathered surface. And eventually he developed a technology of mining. Flint mining and toolmaking together made up an impressively complex enterprise. Finding the buried veins, digging the pits, bringing the flint to the surface, turning it into tools of quality, all made for an operation beyond the capacities of a single man or family. Labour had to be organized on a large scale, sometimes of quite substantial dimensions. Several prehistoric mines and associated factories exist in Europe; one such enterprise recently discovered near Sélédin, in France, is believed to have furnished almost half of all the neolithic axes in Brittany. It covered more than 250 acres and had not only a quarry dug into a bed of fine-grained dolerite but working spaces for cracking, trimming and polishing the quarried rock.

Even more impressive is the mining and manufacturing complex at Grimes Graves in Norfolk in eastern England (*page 86*). The mines were in use for centuries, from early neolithic days down to the middle of the Bronze Age, and they must have produced an astronomical number of tools; examples of their work have turned up all over the British Isles. The miners at Grimes Graves dug scores of pits, some of them 30 feet deep, down through layers of sand and chalk. They were choosy about their flint. At one site they dug through a seam of apparently perfectly good flint to reach a second seam below.

The miners left heaps of debris in worked-out mine

A whole deer antler (top), an antler with most of its tines removed (centre) and an ox shoulder blade (bottom) served neolithic man for digging ditches, burial tombs and mines. The full antler was used to rake the earth, the partial antler to loosen and pry out flint and other stones. The ox bone served as a shovel.

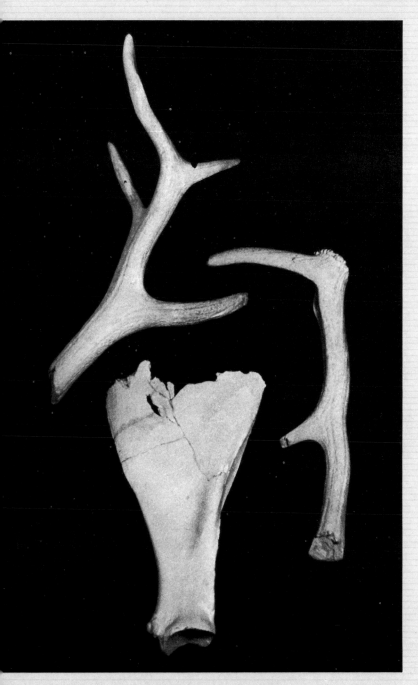

shafts and around the mines on the chipping floors, where they turned the raw flint into tools. Thousands of mining tools that they used and abandoned have been found—picks of deer antler or ox bone, shovels made of the shoulder blades of oxen, antler hammers and rakes. The antlers and ox bones were too brittle to have been swung like modern metal picks; hammer marks at their butt ends indicate that they were driven into cracks in the chalk seam, then worked up and down to loosen blocks of chalk or the bits of flint embedded in it. Fragments of charcoal show that the miners lit their deep galleries with torches; some soot-stained round chalk cups that survive were probably used as oil lamps. There is no evidence, like fruit pits or gnawed ox bones, to indicate that the men ate while labouring in the galleries, so it is supposed that they worked regular shifts and came up for their meals. To get up and down they obviously had some kind of ladder, probably made of a notched tree trunk or knotted rope. The scale of the work and the competence reflected in the construction of the pits and galleries would seem to prove that the miners were not simply local farmers and herdsmen taking time off from their usual pursuits but a separate group of full-time workers, possibly even with further specialization within that group. Some men may have dug the flint out of the mines, while others, working on the chipping floors, may have transformed it into great quantities of tools that were evidently traded far and wide.

Families no less than industries had a division of labour, with the responsibilities probably dictated by custom. Earliest European myths and legends—such as the Greek tales of Persephone and Demeter, of

Mining Flint in Ancient England

In this imaginary cross section of a mine, similar to one excavated at Grimes Graves in eastern England, a dozen men co-operate in the task of extracting and chipping flint, the material used for axes and other major cutting tools of the Neolithic Age.

At the bottom of a shaft some 20 feet below the earth's surface, one man pushes a deer-antler pick into a wall of chalk to loosen a nodule of flint. On a gallery about 10 feet above him, two more men crouch (*right*) as they tunnel into another seam of flint. The miners in the centre load wicker baskets with flint lumps, which will be hoisted upwards by one of the two men holding the ropes above the pit. To the left another man ascends the ladder from the shaft to the grassy downs above, where two workmen sit on boulders (*right*), chipping blocks of flint into crude tool shapes, and two more carry away baskets of debris to dump on a trash heap in the distance.

Zeus and Hera or of Artemis and Actaeon—suggest a matriarchal order or at least a female-orientated society, where the mother may have ranked as head of the household and descent and inheritance were reckoned through her line. But no archaeological evidence survives to prove the point. By late megalithic times more men than women were buried in elaborate graves, which may indicate that male domination was beginning to establish itself. Presumably in the earliest days the division of labour, as it is in most Stone Age cultures today, made the men responsible for land clearance and ploughing and for ensuring the meat supply by hunting and herding. The women probably provided other food by picking wild plants and growing grain and beans. Children too young to work or to hunt may have been assigned to shoo birds off the crops, or they may simply have sat at the feet of the old men, listening to tales of the past. The older women, predecessors perhaps of medieval witches, might have roamed the fields and woods looking for medicinal herbs or hallucinogenic mushrooms or ingredients for a brew to combat sterility or impotence.

Although one can only speculate about the social structure of prehistoric villages, it can be surmised that the society was tribal, with a head man taking the lead in the group's affairs but with a consensus taken on most major matters. The chances are that the whole community met in assembly when an important decision had to be made, involving, for example, a move to a new place or the choice of a site for a megalith.

The building of megaliths was not, in fact, the only large-scale construction undertaken by neolithic man. Southern Britain contains dozens of large earthen circles—generally called causewayed camps, or occasionally bank-and-ditch monuments—that were built as early as 3000 B.C., predating most of the British stone circles by at least two or three centuries. The causewayed camps are among the oldest surviving monuments in England; and a segment of the middle neolithic culture of Britain was for a time called the Windmill Hill Culture, after the site near Avebury where the first causewayed camp was found. Over the ages these sites became hallowed; evidently the populations of many villages or seminomadic tribes of herdsmen gathered there on special occasions to mark the turning of the seasons or to commemorate some event important to the group. Carbon dating of the debris found in some of the ditches—enormous quantities of animal bone—indicates that the camps were at least periodically in use over a great many centuries.

A causewayed camp had one to four oval or circular ditches, more or less concentric, with embankments on the inner sides. The ditches were not continuous but broken at irregular intervals by causeways, or ramps of earth; some have post holes at the sides, indicating that they may once have held gateways. The constructions are not technically megalithic because they are made of earth rather than huge stones, but in their size and in their circular and concentric layout they anticipate the craving for monumentality that was to find expression later in the massive stone structures such as Avebury and Stonehenge itself. The causewayed camps are so solidly and skilfully built that they imply a long familiarity with large-scale construction.

When these early monuments were first discovered about 1900, it was assumed that they were primarily defensive works. This theory held for years until

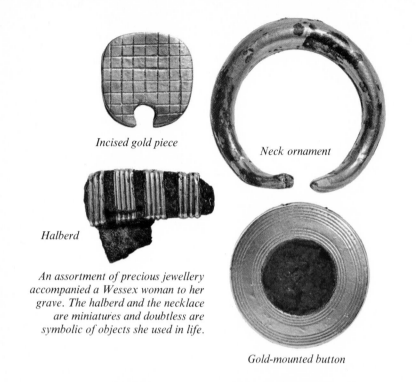

Incised gold piece

Neck ornament

Halberd

An assortment of precious jewellery accompanied a Wessex woman to her grave. The halberd and the necklace are miniatures and doubtless are symbolic of objects she used in life.

Gold-mounted button

Buried Treasures

As the Early Bronze Age advanced, gifts to accompany the departed to their megalithic graves, and the life beyond, became ever more elaborate —a reflection not only of man's ever-increasing skill and affluence but also of his broadened contacts.

The objects shown here, all of gold and amber and dating to about the middle of the Second Millennium B.C., were found in graves in Wessex, England. But the gold was imported from Ireland and the amber is likely to have come from the Baltic.

Although tribal chieftains of different cultures sometimes exchanged gifts of finished objects (*lower left*), the raw materials were usually imported so that local craftsmen could then fashion them to suit local tastes. For example, the warriors' dazzling ornaments (*right*) were made by applying thin sheets of gold to shaped foundations of wood, leather or some other substantial material.

A pure gold beaker found in a Cornish grave was ribbed after the fashion of corded pottery. It is three and a half inches high, and may have been a Mycenaean gift to a British chief.

A gold belt buckle (left) and a similarly incised gold breastplate (below) adorned a warrior's grave in Wiltshire. Neither is shown to scale: the belt buckle is roughly three inches by three inches, and the breastplate is eight and a half inches across.

A gold pommel mount for a dagger, with designs incised on top and sides, was found in a Dorset grave—with a supply of dagger blades and an axe. It measures two inches in diameter.

some scholar pointed out that it would have been absurd, even for the neolithic mentality, to build a defensive work and leave large holes in it every 20 yards or so. It is now thought that the camps were assembly points, fairgrounds or possibly religious centres, where different tribes or clans gathered to perform religious rites, marry off their young, exchange gossip and goods, and in general express their sense of community and their links to their inherited traditions. The surrounding banks would have provided a magnificent grandstand for looking down on the central area, itself a most imposing stage; the monument at Windmill Hill measures 270 by 210 feet, and others are even larger. The ceremonies held at Windmill Hill may have prefigured those staged later in more grandiose form at the towering megalithic sites of Avebury and Stonehenge.

Whatever the ceremonies did encompass, they rarely included burials. Few human bones are found in the causewayed camps. Almost all the material evidence of burials is in separate neolithic tombs. Although the tombs themselves are smaller than the causewayed camps, they reveal a great deal about neolithic life—through neolithic death. For the tombs contain more than skeletons; they also have preserved tools, weapons and other artifacts that were buried with the dead.

Valuable as they are, these objects must be treated warily as clues to prehistoric daily life. Neolithic man did not seal up the tombs as time capsules to document his era for the benefit of generations to come. It is more likely that he intended to hide them forever from the eyes of living man, that the graves and the grave goods were intended to be useful to the dead, perhaps as personal belongings in the other world, perhaps as offerings to the mysterious powers out there. Grave goods were a special kind of luxury item and may not have resembled exactly the mundane objects of daily life. Many of the stone and bronze axes and daggers found in the graves were evidently made for burial, because they had not been used to cut anything on earth.

The fact that he built more lasting homes for the dead than for the living does not prove that neolithic man was obsessed with death. The Egyptians did likewise, yet their wall paintings and writings show they were as eager as any people for life. There are no megalithic wall paintings, only the heavy, gloom-filled monuments with their abstract and enigmatic carvings. But the fact is that today the monuments stand stripped down by time. Thousands of years ago they may have been gaily decorated. The piles of animal bones left beside them, which must be the remains of funerary feasts, indicate that the passing of souls to the beyond may have been as much an occasion for rejoicing as for sorrow. The Irish wake, one of the oldest of traditions, could have evolved out of such observances.

But how did the tombs themselves evolve? Nobody has the answer. Some scholars once believed that immigrants to northern Europe had been accustomed to cutting their tombs into the Mediterranean cliffsides of Mycenae and Crete; when they came to a new country with no handy cliffs of soft rock, they created artificial hills with artificial rock-lined caves dug into them. This assumption, with its companion diffusionist theory that the source of all culture lay in the East, has fallen out of favour. The burial customs of the megalithic age, most scholars now believe, rep-

Pottery and stone vessels frequently turn up among the ruins of Early Bronze Age burials. The handled cup at top, three and a half inches high, was carved from shale. The two incense cups, perforated to allow fumes to dissipate, have been decorated with knobs and impressions of cord in the wet clay.

resent the flowering of a tradition that goes back to antiquity on the same soil.

One supporting bit of evidence is a miniature rock chamber built in the Dordogne Valley of southwestern France in Magdalenian times—over 1,500 miles from Mycenae and Crete, and 10,000 years earlier than those civilizations. A woman has been found buried there, her bones sprinkled with red ochre (perhaps to recall the flush of life), with 70 deer teeth strung like beads around her neck.

Further evidence comes from some campsites off the coast of Brittany, where hunter-gatherers buried their dead under heaps of stones in the middens, or garbage dumps, adjoining their dwelling places. Perhaps the stones were piled on top of the dead to protect them from scavenging animals. In any case, it has been argued that neolithic immigrants arriving from the south adopted this burial custom, and as their capability and ambitions grew they gradually made the heaps more grandiose.

Some of them moved on across the Channel to England. But those who did at first built earthen barrows, not megaliths, though megaliths had been built in Brittany as early as 4500 B.C., well over a half millennium before the first known barrows in Britain.

The barrows were elongated heaps of earth and pebbles, which might be 300 feet long or more, with as many as 50 bodies buried near one end. As the barrows now stand, the bones simply lie in the earth; but originally they were probably placed in enclosures of wood or turf that eventually collapsed under the weight of the mound above. When the builders began using stone instead of wood for the walls and roofs, the megalithic tomb had come to Britain.

During the long centuries when megaliths served

as tombs, funeral practices changed again and again. Sometimes it was customary to bury the bodies, at other times to burn them. When they were buried they might be stretched out, or they might be placed in a crouching or sitting position. Bones might be laid out in orderly patterns or piled up helter-skelter. And in some of the tombs the bodies apparently were not buried until some time after death; the corpses must have lain exposed, perhaps until all the flesh had rotted away, before they were ceremonially transferred to the tombs. The tombs might be used for short periods or for long periods. Most of them eventually were sealed up tight, either by piling immense weights of earth over them or by rolling up a heavy stone to block the entrance.

Some mysterious powers were evidently thought to inhere in the skeletons of the dead. Many graves are missing certain bones like jaws and thighs, which have always been favourites for divination and magic rites. Among the graves found near Paris many skulls have been neatly trepanned—an operation in which a disc is cut from the skull. Although in some instances the operation seems to have been performed on living persons, possibly to repair head injuries or to cure sickness, in others it apparently was performed on the skulls of the dead. The excised bits of bone must have been prized as charms or good-luck pieces, for bone amulets have been found lying beside other skeletons in many graves.

Animal bones found in front of tombs indicate that there were sacrifices connected with the funerals, probably of beasts appropriate to the life style of the deceased or his fellows. In places where herding and stockbreeding were the base of the economy, the bull seems to have been the favourite sacrificial animal. In

Inside a passage grave at Fourknocks, Ireland, a mound 60 feet in diameter and 12 feet high, the walls of the central chamber are lined with massive stones. Some of them bear carvings of chevron and diamond patterns such as those on the lintel at centre left.

other places, where the community depended more on hunting, deer, pig and elk have been found.

There also is some slight evidence that megalithic man practised human sacrifice. But most deaths seem to have come from natural causes. Although neolithic people had weapons and knew how to use them —one skeleton found in a grave near Paris has an arrowhead lodged in its skull—not until the middle of the Bronze Age, when megalith building had ceased and swords and daggers began to replace axes and arrowheads in the graves, does it appear that the weapons were used primarily to kill human beings. In the Neolithic Age axes were for chopping trees and arrows for felling wild game. Perhaps there was a little ceremonial head-hunting, an occasional skirmish with cattle rustlers or battles on the order of the ones fought to this day in the mountains of New Guinea—primarily to show off the courage of the young braves. Men are wounded and even killed in these battles, but the fighting is always called off at sunset, and everyone goes home to his village and resumes the routine of his daily life. In some societies such combats serve the purpose of working off excess energy in the young. In others they are thought to have some kind of religious connotation, the significance of which is long lost.

The religions of neolithic man also remain something of a mystery; but some intriguing hints survive among the artifacts. One of the most striking collections turned up in a pit at the Grimes Graves flint mines. On a pedestal of chalk blocks at the right side of a gallery entrance was a carved figure, about four inches high, of a grotesquely fat, apparently pregnant woman. To the left of the figure was a carved chalk phallus and a heap of chalk balls. Facing this assemblage was a mass of blocks of mined flint looking like a triangular altar with a chalk cup at the base of the triangle facing the female figure. Seven deer antler picks were piled on the altar, if altar it was.

This assemblage was not made at random, and its purpose can be guessed. The pit whose entrance was thus decorated was dug into a seam of chalk that did not contain much flint. The sexual connotations of the shrine indicate an attempt to cajole the Earth Goddess into being more fruitful on this spot and giving birth to more workable flint to reward the frustrated miners for their toil.

Other representations of the same goddess occur elsewhere, sometimes with a serpent consort, sometimes with other mysterious symbols twisting and writhing their way across the walls of megalithic monuments. The men who created them clearly felt that they had access to hidden powers that, through the use of proper rites and gestures, could be used to assure their well-being and to ward off evil.

Whether religious rites were confined to community ceremonies or were also participated in at home is not known. In the lakes of the Swiss Alps a number of sunken villages have been found in a state of almost perfect preservation since the rising water covered them three or four thousand years ago. The houses have yielded a rich collection of axes, knives, nets, fishing rods, bowls, ladles, troughs—all kinds of household apparatus, but not a single cult object. Such houses at a later stage of human development would have been full of sacred objects, like figurines of Isis or Aphrodite or the Virgin Mary. Perhaps the figurines of the Earth Goddess in the lake houses were hurriedly snatched away when the floods came. Perhaps, on the other hand, neolithic man regarded his relations with divinity as a social and community matter, associated with the worship of the dead and with projects for the community's good, rather than as a part of his private life.

It has been argued that the very shape of the megaliths symbolized certain religious ideas. According to a view popularized by archaeologist V. Gordon Childe, who excavated Skara Brae (*pages 99-103*), the first megalith builders were missionaries who brought new ideas of divinity and of the soul of man to Western Europe. According to his theory, the variations in shape and construction of the megaliths corresponded to variations in sects from region to region. This theory was shaken in 1954 when a hitherto unsuspected megalithic complex was discovered near Barnenez on the north coast of Brittany.

The discovery of Barnenez was one of those accidents that mark the history of many megaliths. A road contractor in the area thought he might find suitable material in two long grass-covered knolls overlooking the sea. The knolls indeed turned out to be filled with high-grade gravel and large lumps of rock. The contractor had completely destroyed one of the knolls and was at work on the other when the authorities were alerted that he might be destroying a national treasure. No one knows what was in the mound he destroyed, but when archaeologists got to the other mound in the nick of time they made a major find: no less than eleven passage graves, all side by side. Some of them have since proved to be among the oldest man-made structures on earth.

The graves were built during two periods a couple of hundred years apart in the Fifth Millennium; and one fascinating fact about them is that, although all

An ample mother goddess made of chalk, the expendable material from which flint is extracted, once watched over an unproductive shaft at Grimes Graves, a neolithic flint mine in eastern England. Her imaginative creator set the four-and-a-half-inch statuette next to a chalk phallus, evidently in the prayerful hope of improving the output of the mine.

are passage graves, no two of them are exactly alike. Some graves use megaliths as construction blocks, others use stone walls with the megaliths as non-functional ornaments in front of them. They are orientated in slightly different directions. Some have decorative carvings, while others do not. Some of them have flat-roofed chambers, others have corbelled roofs. It would seem that the architectural forms were chosen according to the taste of the builders, just as they are in modern cemeteries. Major architectural differences—between gallery and passage graves—may indeed be cultural, but lesser differences in layout and construction seem to have been easily tolerated by the megalith builders.

The acid soil of Brittany has long since disintegrated most of the bones that were laid in the tombs of Barnenez, so it is not known how many funerals actually took place there. In tombs elsewhere the bones have been perfectly preserved and the number of individuals buried can be counted. At Tinkinswood, near Cardiff in Wales, for example, there are fragmented bones of 50 persons, both male and female, both young and old, and apparently spread over several generations.

The Tinkinswood tomb is a roughly rectangular chamber, walled and roofed with limestone slabs and set at the eastern end of a barrow some 130 feet long. One archaeologist estimates that it would have taken more than 50 able-bodied men one year to put up this impressive edifice; thus Tinkinswood must have been a community of considerable size. So this and other megalithic burial tombs raise a fascinating question: where were the other members of the community buried when they died? Unless, as seems unlikely, every last human suddenly took off, leaving a ghost town and a ghostly megalith behind, most of the people in the community must have been dumped into shallow graves when they died, or left to rot on the surface of the ground. In any event, since there is only this one megalith in the immediate neighbourhood, most of the people in the settlement must not have been so honoured when they died.

It would seem, therefore, that there were some class distinctions in early megalithic society. Some people seem to have merited having their remains put into splendid monuments, and others did not. Certain of the privileged dead were expected to pass on, with the help of sacrifices and grave offerings, to a fairer land in another life—perhaps to such a place as the Fortunate Isles (which occur in both Irish and Greek myth), where heroes were rewarded for a strenuous life on earth by perpetual ease thereafter.

What entitled a neolithic settler to such a privileged afterlife? Not achievement certainly, for there are infants in some of these tombs. Presumably it was a hereditary privilege, belonging to the family of some renowned ancestor who had been able to endow all his offspring with a special divine blessing, like Father Abraham in the Bible. Or it could be that some families laboured to provide tombs for themselves and their descendants, while others did not. A study made at the chamber tomb of Lanhill, in Wiltshire in southern England, showed strong resemblances among the bones of the nine individuals buried there. Seven of the skulls have a rare bone formation known as the Wormian ossicle, a growth known to be hereditary. It seems probable that Lanhill was a family vault.

The question then arises: if there was favoured treatment in death, did it follow favoured treatment in

Giving the effect of some gigantic fingerprints, concentric arcs and rounded arches cover part of the wall of a tomb in Gavrinis, Brittany, built in the Third Millennium B.C.

Pictorial Puzzles from the Past

In most of the nearly 15,000 megalithic tombs of Western Europe the walls are entirely bare of ornament. But about 200 of them, chiefly in Brittany and Ireland, contain remarkable mural decorations whose meanings elude modern scholars.

The decorations are thought to have been done before the megaliths were set in place, and were apparently fashioned by hammer and chisel of unusually hard stone. The designs are sometimes incised, sometimes in low relief. A few are faintly representational, but most are geometric patterns and would seem at first glance to have been intended as purely ornamental. Some archaeologists believe these designs are stylized symbols; a circle, for example, may have signified the eye of a deity.

The difficulty of deciphering the meanings of the wall carvings is compounded by the fact that later generations occasionally renovated the tombs or added symbols to the walls to reflect new religious beliefs and new fashions. The designs thus remain open to as many interpretations as may strike the beholder's fancy.

Linear drawings—rare in megalithic murals—suggest an axehead, waves and a boat prow on a slab at Petit-Mont, Brittany. The feet are thought to have been a relatively modern intrusion.

Archaeologists have detected either a cooking pot with wheat protruding from its top or a mother goddess guarding a departed soul in this engraving from Luffang, Brittany.

Zigzag lines—a motif frequently used by early peoples to symbolize serpents —form striking parallel rows on an interior wall of the main chamber of the tomb at Fourknocks, Ireland.

Spirals are joined in a triskelion, or three-branched figure, on a slab at a grave site at New Grange, Ireland, the most richly decorated of all neolithic tombs in Europe and the British Isles.

Either the sun or an eye may be signified in this carving in a curbstone of a retaining wall that was built to protect the base of a burial mound at Dowth, County Meath, Ireland.

life? Did the families who had the right to a megalithic tomb and a glorious afterlife enjoy any special
favours while they were passing through the earthly
phase of their existence? The evidence is ambiguous,
but in general the answer appears to be no.

In the tombs at Xemxija on Malta lie the bones of
a number of young men who were apparently healthy
enough at death but whose bones lack the deep
grooves caused by the attachment of powerful mus-
cles. Were these young men gilded youths who had
nothing to do but loll around while others toiled to
put up towering tombs for their precious bones?

If so, they are the exception. And whatever the evidence of the tombs, the evidence of the few surviving
dwelling places elsewhere on the Continent indicates
an egalitarian society in which no one lived on a
grander scale than his neighbours. The lake houses of
Switzerland are all about the same size and furnished
in about the same way. At Barkjaer, in East Jutland,
the settlement is composed of two long parallel wood-
en buildings, each divided into 26 identical single-
room apartments, all as orderly and uniform as a
barracks. So are the stone houses at Skara Brae. Some
of the walrus hunters and the sheepherders of Skara
Brae may have ended up in the magnificent passage
grave of Maes Howe nine miles away; but while they
lived, they fared no better than their neighbours in
that inhospitable land.

A basically egalitarian society, then, in which certain elements had more prestige than others but no
one person had out-of-the-ordinary material com-
forts, would have been the ideal community for
erecting megalithic monuments. For the task must
have demanded some effort from every able-bodied
member of the populace. It was once assumed that
large-scale public works demanded a rigidly hierarchical society, with an authoritarian government
controlling a cowed population of slaves. Fanciful
writers have described aristocrats of the Beaker People or other invaders imposing their rule on the
backward native populations and dragooning them
into forced labour, with overseers cracking their
whips. Kings of Wessex are depicted superintending
vast armies of slaves to build Stonehenge, just as the
pharaohs of Egypt did to build the pyramids. This is
all moonshine. A king in Wessex—if there were kings
in Wessex in prehistoric times, and there is no con-
clusive evidence that there were—would have found
it hard to keep a big labour force under his rule unless
he imprisoned his workers, because they could simply wander off. In Egypt the pharaoh's subjects had
little choice: if they did not want to work on the pyramids all they could do was flee to the desert, where
they surely would starve or die of thirst. But anyone
who did not want to work on Stonehenge had only to
take off with his wife, a sow, an axe and a bag of seed
—off into the trackless forest to join another
settlement or start one of his own.

More likely, it was not force but a sense of community that called forth the tremendous efforts of
the megalith builders. These monuments can be seen
as the spontaneous outpouring of a whole people's
energy, with everyone—young and old, men and
women—pitching in. The work must have gone forward in an atmosphere of mass enthusiasm and freely
accepted discipline, with every citizen of the community working on the project—possibly under the
guidance of priests or master builders—and proud to
be contributing to a monument that would stand forever to the glory of his people and his gods.

Skara Brae: A Neolithic Village Revealed

A flagstone walk leads between two stone-walled houses of Skara Brae towards the dunes that hid the settlement for millennia.

A savage storm lashed the Orkney Islands off the coast of Scotland in the winter of 1850, ripping up the sand dunes in its path. When it subsided, the astonished residents of Mainland Island beheld a cluster of stone houses whose existence they had never suspected. Subsequent excavation has proved it to be a neolithic village that had lain untouched beneath the sand for thousands of years.

The village, now known as Skara Brae (Scottish words meaning hilly dunes), is remarkable on two counts. One is that it is the most fully preserved neolithic site yet found anywhere in Europe. The other is that it is built entirely of stone—not only the houses, but also their furnishings. Stone does not lend itself to carbon dating, and the other relics in the town are only now in the process of being dated. But the stone tools and the pottery found in the houses correspond to similar artifacts known to have been used elsewhere in the British Isles during the Third Millennium B.C.

The exposed interiors of two of Skara Brae's houses—designated Nos. 4 and 5 by archaeologists—show the stone slabs that served not only a

walls but also as pavements, steps and even as bedsteads and storage bins.

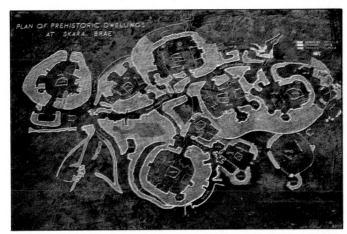

A plaque at the ancient site's entrance shows visitors its layout.

A World of Stone

The settlement of Skara Brae consisted of 10 stone houses connected or separated by stone walls and linked by stone alleys. They were furnished with stone beds, benches and storage cubicles containing stone axes and knives. Some of the beds had tall posts, also of stone, which probably held skin canopies to keep out the northern cold.

Each house consisted of a single room with rounded corners, measuring about 20 by 21 feet. Peat ashes were found in the hearths, along with the remains of cattle and sheep bones, indicating that the people lived by herding. The roofs —almost the only part of the construction to have collapsed—are thought to have been skins laid over whalebone rafters.

Apparently the people abandoned their town abruptly; this is suggested by a string of beads dropped in a passage and by partly gnawed bones left by a bedside. It may be that Skara Brae's inhabitants fled from a storm as savage as the one that in modern times exposed their site anew.

The village of Skara Brae, which thousands of years ago sheltered several generations of neolithic families, today lies unearthed but partially

protected from the chill and blustering northern elements by the grassy dunes that blanket the ruins and spread down to the edge of the sea.

Chapter Five: Raising Boulders to the Sky

Because the megalith builders usually left the stones they worked with in their natural state, it has been tempting to conclude that they were rough, artless men with a rule-of-thumb mastery for getting big stones to stand upright. But a careful look at any one of the principal monuments shows that their builders were much more accomplished. They were ingenious engineers capable of working out complex mathematical calculations and solving with sheer muscle power problems that would be considered formidable even in this machine-powered age. More significant, they were true innovators. Without books or museums to look to for inspiration, they created something new under the sun; the first structures designed to last forever.

Modern experiments in erecting a large stone with only the tools available to ancient man make megalith building seem relatively easy. A dozen average-sized archaeologists using this primitive kind of equipment have been able to raise and set on end a stone weighing several tons. But building a megalithic monument was a much more complicated matter than simply standing a large stone on end. As the soil settled and storms swept over it, such a precariously balanced monolith would soon have toppled over. The megalith builders set each of these enormous boulders into a footing in the earth.

But more was involved than just settling huge stones in the ground. The construction of a mega-

A 19th Century artist's effort to show how massive menhirs were moved was both right and wrong according to modern research. He was correct in assuming the stones had to be moved on rollers, but he shows only 11 men hauling each stone with a single rope on level ground and up a grade; at least 1,000 men and countless ropes would have been needed.

lithic monument was perhaps the most important single event of each generation of a neolithic community, and its planning must have involved long and careful consideration. There must have been a meeting of the whole population, or at least of the older and wiser men and women. Some sort of divine sanction—a favourable omen or a seemingly miraculous happening—might have been necessary before the final decision to go ahead. Nor would work on a major monument have begun without a careful study of all possibilities. Suggested designs were probably scratched on the ground. Monuments in neighbouring regions were studied, and perhaps even one of the community's leaders travelled across the channel to get ideas from especially impressive and well-known megalithic centres like Stonehenge in Britain or the miles of standing stones at Carnac, on the coast of Brittany. Meanwhile the building project, however ambitious, would have to be integrated with the community's other activities so as not to disrupt the daily life of the village.

Once this preliminary planning was done, the megalith builders would be faced with essentially technical decisions, the first concerning where their monument was to stand. Perhaps they recognized a site as being propitious, even sacred, when something extraordinary took place there. A god might appear to the chief of the community; a stream might gush from a rock; a milk-white cow might lie down to rest. Or the wise men might point out some astronomical significance of a piece of land: the sun rises just so over a certain hill at the time of the summer solstice.

It might of course have been as simple a consideration as the fact that it was a good place for a monument. Monuments like the great mound-covered

Enduring Feats of Engineering

Engineering skill, as well as brawn, went into the construction of Europe's monuments. At New Grange, a tomb in Ireland, the builders prevented the roofs of the underground chambers and passages from caving in by means of corbelling (*below*), a stone-laying technique that creates a supportive arch. Stonehenge's lofty lintels were secured on top of the uprights by tenons and mortises (*right*), a system of interlocking prongs and indentations. The aim of these and other ingenious devices was to make the monuments durable—and the methods have had remarkable success.

Even after 5,000 years, the two-story-high underground central chamber at New Grange remains intact, its sides still narrowing towards the top

An upright and a fallen lintel still bear the tenon (bump on top of upright) and mortise (indentation in lintel) that once locked them together. The upright bulges slightly so that to a viewer looking up at it, it appears straight.

A skywards view of the lintels at Stonehenge, once part of its impressive Sarsen Circle, shows the subtle curve that was made during the cutting of each stone. The lintels, mounted end to end, form a smooth arc.

passage graves of the Boyne Valley in Ireland, which were built on top of rises, must have been intended to be seen and admired for miles around. Like medieval churches in European villages, such strikingly situated tombs were meant to be focal points for the life of the community. The farmer or herdsman in the fields, even the children playing in the village would always be aware of the looming presence of the monuments, reinforcing their sense of identity as a people and their loyalty to their forebears.

Perhaps the most logical reason for choosing a site would be that that was where the stones were. The simple chamber tombs of Denmark and northern Germany seem to have been constructed with the stones readily at hand. But frequently the site was picked and then the stones were selected elsewhere—in the case of Stonehenge, nearly 20 miles away. No doubt Stonehenge's sarsens were chosen for their monolithic mass as well as for some now-forgotten mystic quality. Other building materials appear to have been used for aesthetic reasons. The builders of the cyclopean temple of Hagar Qim in Malta, for example, had the choice of two kinds of limestone, the coralline and the softer globigerina. The latter, with its warm golden-brown colouring, is the more attractive to modern eyes; so although it was less durable and although they had to cross the island to get it and then haul it back over the rocky hills, the Maltese used globigerina for the entire temple.

While the stones used for most megaliths were boulders found on the surface, some were quarried out of bedrock or cliffsides. One suggested method was discovered in the mid-20th Century by the Norwegian anthropologist Thor Heyerdahl. In the 1950s Heyerdahl was studying the hundreds of gigantic statues that have made Easter Island famous and have puzzled generations of explorers. Clearly these statues had been quarried out of the dark-grained stone in the island's interior. Work in these quarries had ceased by the end of the 17th Century; but some memory of how the work had been accomplished had been kept alive through folklore by the original artisans' descendants.

Heyerdahl rounded up a half-dozen islanders to see if they could demonstrate the technique. Indeed they could. They climbed confidently to the old work sites, which were still littered with stone picks where they had been dropped 300 years earlier. The islanders grasped the picks, which Heyerdahl thought resembled "gigantic eyeteeth with sharp points", held them like daggers and began to strike the surface of the rock. They chipped away to the rhythm of a stonecutters' song that had come down with their ancestral legends. "They sang and hewed", writes Heyerdahl, "hewed and sang. One tall old man at the end of the line was so inspired that he danced and swayed his hips as he sang and hewed". It was slow work, each blow making barely a mark on the hard surface. But little by little their chipping began to wear away the rock. When their picks grew dull they struck them against other picks, producing a new point "as easily as a clerk sharpens a pencil". Eventually they cut away a huge block of the kind from which their ancestors had carved the famous statues.

The ancient Easter Islanders would have completed a statue at the quarry site and then moved it to where it was to be erected, a task that must have required general mobilization of the population. Heyerdahl did not attempt to move the newly quarried block; instead he managed to duplicate the feat on a smaller scale. He persuaded 180 islanders to join together in a carnival atmosphere and, using manila ropes, move some of the fallen giant figures back into place. So it must have been in neolithic Europe, with whole villages or groups of villages united for mass enterprises like hauling the 40-ton sarsen stones 20 miles over the downs to Stonehenge, perhaps to the sound of drums, horns, pipes and the chanting of traditional work songs.

After the megalith builders had hauled their stones to a construction site, their work was far from finished. In some cases, nature had provided the required dimensions and no further shaping was needed; the so-called male and female twins facing each other down the long Avenue at Avebury in southern England are examples of such ready-made forms. In other instances, the stones had been broken into the correct sizes and shapes where they had been found, sometimes by tedious chipping away and sometimes by alternately heating and cooling them until they cracked (*pages 122-123*). But many of the stones had knobs or bulges or awkward angles that had to be smoothed down; and these finishing touches had to be applied at the site.

The amount of additional dressing done on the stones depended on conceptions and dogmas that remain mysterious to modern investigators. Some boulders were simply left with the rough surface that wind and weather had provided; others were worked down to more or less flat planes; some rare stones were symbolically decorated with the loops and lines that form the repertory of megalithic art. Such decorating, done on stone with stone tools, must have seemed an interminable process; the air around the monuments must have rung with the stonecutters' blows, day after day, for years on end.

Several different techniques were used to decorate the stones, and a variety of tools dug up by archaeologists gives an idea of how the designs were applied. Lines could be engraved with sharp stone blades (chisels) or with bronze blades in later megalithic times. Surfaces could be made fairly smooth by pounding them with round stone mauls, or they could be pocked by repeated blows with a heavy stone hammer or tapped with an oval maul to give the stones patterns of concave impressions. (Archaeologists have found stone hammers drilled to take a wooden handle and still bearing traces of the resin that held hammer and handle firmly together.) Decorated stones were sometimes combined with plain stones, as in the great passage grave at New Grange, Ireland. But in a tomb like New Grange it seems clear that not all the designs were meant to be seen, at least not by the living. Here and at similar tombs some of the decorated stones are hidden in the dark interior, and some are concealed behind other stones. Presumably what was important to the builders was some magic power inherent in the design, rather than a dazzling display for the faithful.

When the huge stones had been suitably shaped and decorated, the megalith builders were ready for the next stage of the operation: raising the stones into position. This herculean task must have involved another general mobilization of the community's able-bodied workers, perhaps with feasting, dancing, music and solemn religious rites to accompany the daring and portentous act of raising a mighty part of the earth to stand against the sky.

From careful investigation at Stonehenge, prehis-

A Modern Analysis of Some Very Old Maths

Britain is dotted with ring-shaped monuments whose ground plans appear crude—at first glance. Closer scrutiny reveals that they are perfectly symmetrical; in fact, their very oddness seems not only intentional but the product of careful calculations. But what those calculations were is a puzzle that tantalizes scholars.

Alexander Thom, a retired professor of engineering science, has measured and pondered over some 600 of these curious rings and observed that three basic forms appear repeatedly: (1) circles with one side flattened; (2) ellipses; and (3) ovoids. He has also worked out what might have been the geometric methods of the monuments' designers; at right are three of his reconstructions.

Thom has calculated that these prehistoric mathematicians worked with a basic unit exactly 2.72 feet long, which he calls a megalithic yard. This unit, he feels, was used in laying out monuments hundreds of miles apart, suggesting a central bureau of standards that dispensed yardsticks of machine-like precision. Thom contends that the ancient geometers not only were precise but also preferred simplicity: as the ellipse at right illustrates, they devised near-circles with circumferences that could be measured in multiples of two and a half megalithic yards, thus avoiding complex fractions.

Thom also thinks that the Stone Age geometers may have known what the Greek philosopher Pythagoras —born 2,000 years later—is generally credited with discovering: that a triangle with sides of certain proportions will always have right angles in it (3 X 4 X 5; 5, 12, 13; 12, 35, 37; etc.). A pair of "Pythagorean" triangles figures in the design of the ovoid at right.

Why the monument builders were so fascinated with maths is as unknown as the exact purposes these peculiar rings served. Perhaps these early geometers used the structures as observatories or as shrines in a religion based on mathematics; or the rings may simply be permanent versions of successful experiments in geometry.

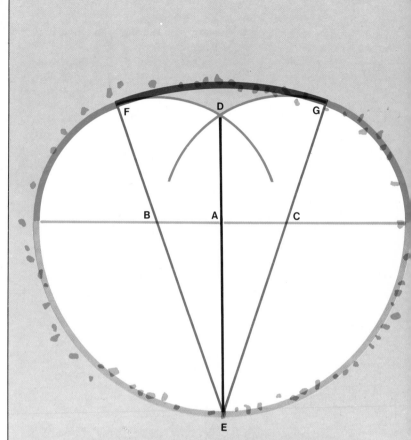

A flattened circle of stones (*grey shapes*) called Long Meg, in northern England, attests to one megalithic architect's ingenuity with a compass and some marking pins. To construct it, he may have begun by describing part of a large circle (*orange*) with its centre at A; he then marked its diameter (*green*). Next he divided the diameter into three equal parts and left markers at points B and C. From B and C he drew two smaller arcs (*blue*); from the point where those arcs intersected each other, at point D, he drew a perpendicular line (*black*) through the centre of the diameter. Where the perpendicular line met the bottom of the circle, at point E, he anchored his compass and drew the last arc (*red*). As his preliminary geometric calculations had indicated, this arc met the other arcs smoothly at points F and G, completing the flattened part of the ring.

The planner of Borrowston Rig in Scotland designed a complete, symmetrical ovoid shape by working with right angles and straight lines. He probably started with a large partial circle (*orange*) with a radius (*broken black line*) 25 MY (megalithic yards) long. Then he extended the radius upwards, to point A, with a line 15.5 MY long (*solid black line*). He now used this extension as the common hypotenuse of two adjacent right-angled triangles (*blue*), their other sides measuring 12.25 and 9.5 MY. He then drew two more radii (*pink*) along the triangles' bases, meeting the outer circle at points B and C. Returning to his triangles, he stood at point A and drew a circle (*green*) with a 15.5 MY radius. This gave him the top of his ovoid shape but left gaps at either side, which he simply closed with straight lines (*red*).

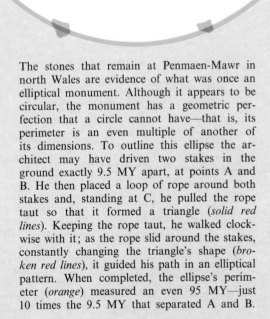

The stones that remain at Penmaen-Mawr in north Wales are evidence of what was once an elliptical monument. Although it appears to be circular, the monument has a geometric perfection that a circle cannot have—that is, its perimeter is an even multiple of another of its dimensions. To outline this ellipse the architect may have driven two stakes in the ground exactly 9.5 MY apart, at points A and B. He then placed a loop of rope around both stakes and, standing at C, he pulled the rope taut so that it formed a triangle (*solid red lines*). Keeping the rope taut, he walked clockwise with it; as the rope slid around the stakes, constantly changing the triangle's shape (*broken red lines*), it guided his path in an elliptical pattern. When completed, the ellipse's perimeter (*orange*) measured an even 95 MY—just 10 times the 9.5 MY that separated A and B.

torians have been able to reconstruct what appears to have been a standard technique for setting up a monumental stone at this and other major megalithic sites. First, a force of workers, using shovels made of wood or perhaps even the shoulder blades of oxen, dug a pit into which the base of stone was to be lowered. The pit was made about two feet larger in diameter than the stone to allow room for last-minute adjustments in its positioning. Its depth was precisely gauged to make sure that the part of the stone to appear above ground would be the proper height. One side of the finished pit formed a ramp that sloped at about a 45-degree angle; the opposite side was a vertical wall faced with wooden stakes to prevent the earth from caving in as the stone was set in place. Excavations have revealed fragments of these stakes still in the ground, and in the disturbed earth around them archaeologists not only have been able to distinguish the shape of the pits themselves but also have remains of the tools that were employed in the operation.

The great stone, lying on its side with base foremost, was then unloaded from its sledge onto more log rollers and pushed and pulled to the ramp side of the pit. Then it was eased over the edge until its centre of gravity was almost over the leading roller. Men using wooden levers then raised the top end, and the entire monolith slid down the ramp, its toe coming to rest against the stakes on the opposite wall. More levering tipped it up from the ramp a few inches; log struts were placed beneath the stone to hold it in position, and still more levering raised it farther. This process—alternately heaving on levers and bracing with struts—was repeated over and over as the stone gradually rose nearly upright.

The stonecutters often shaped the base of such a stone to a blunt point so that it could be pivoted when the moment came to fix it in its final position. Now, as it wobbled in the pit on its point, a couple of hundred men straining on fibre ropes pulled it erect and adjusted it to the position the master builders desired, while others poured earth and rubble into the hole, packing it in tightly. At last the monolith stood firmly in place against the sky. It would take about a year of settling into the soil before the giant pillar was permanently embedded in the earth, ready to stand unmoved for thousands of years.

In some cases there was an even more daring and complex operation ahead: placing the heavy lintels or capstones on top of the upright stones. This heaving of monstrous weights into the air, against every apparent rule of nature, was the accomplishment that more than any other amazed future generations down to the present day. And it must have been a source of particular pride to those who accomplished it.

One way of getting an upper tier of stones in place may have been to drag them up a slope. With the uprights in position, hundreds of workers would set about piling earth and rubble to make a ramp against the standing stones. When completed, it would have formed an artificial hill on which stones could be hauled over log rollers. Adjacent to some dolmens are remains of earthworks that may represent such ramps (they may also be traces of vanished barrows). But there are other monuments—Stonehenge, for example, with its seven-ton lintel stones—where there is no sign of any ramp. At these sites some other device must have been used.

That device may have been an ever-growing support of stones or timbers. A possible clue to how it worked was witnessed by Thor Heyerdahl on Easter Island while he was re-creating the work of the island's statue carvers. Heyerdahl persuaded a team of 12 islanders to restore to its original pedestal a giant statue that had been knocked down during a civil war in the 17th Century. The figure was nearly 10 feet wide across the shoulders and weighed almost 30 tons; it lay face down alongside the wall on which it once had stood.

As in quarrying a massive block with primitive stone picks, the islanders had only ancestral memories to guide them. But they developed a confident skill and an *esprit de corps* as they tackled the project, and the task was completed in 18 days.

It was tricky and dangerous work from the start. Wooden levers were first wedged under one side of the statue and it was tilted a fraction of an inch, just enough to shove some small stones under it. Then it was tilted a fraction more for another layer of stones; then again and again. The construction proceeded like that of a farmer building a dry stone wall. When the pile of stones was a couple of feet high, the levers were moved to the other side of the statue, which was raised in turn and stones packed under it, until the figure was horizontal again. Back went the poles to the other side, the statue was again tilted, and in this way it rose inch by inch on its stony bed. By the ninth day it had risen nearly 12 feet. At this point, notes Heyerdahl, "the weight of the colossus was so great that some of the stones cracked under the pressure like lumps of sugar; a single carelessly placed stone could mean catastrophe".

On the tenth day the recumbent statue was on a level with the wall that had once been its pedestal. The workers started to lever and prod its base forward towards the wall. On the eleventh day they began to raise it into a sloping position by increasing the pile of stones under its head and chest. By the seventeenth day it reached the critical angle, ready to swing upright onto its pedestal. On the next and final day, in one last heave, the islanders prodded it upright. The heap of stones went crashing down in a cloud of dust. The statue wobbled and then stood still on its lordly platform, its brooding face once more overlooking the Pacific.

According to Heyerdahl, this 30-ton figure could be juggled into place by men not normally used to such work only because "every little move was precisely and logically calculated". Such must also have been the case with the megalith builders. A wrong move not only would be a blow to the reputation of the master builders but might crush to death a couple dozen of the local population. And, as the monuments are studied with increasing care, there is mounting evidence that their designers were indeed remarkable technicians. In the New Grange passage grave Irish archaeologists have recently uncovered a whole network of grooved stones forming a drainage system that keeps rain water out of the burial chamber. At Stonehenge the sides of many of the upright pillars swell slightly as they rise to counteract the optical illusion that makes a perfectly perpendicular column appear from the ground to curve inward towards the top. This architectural device for ensuring that the sides of a column look parallel from top to bottom is known by the Greek word *entasis* (meaning swelling), and at one time it was taken for granted that the method was invented by the Greeks—a proof of the elegant ingenuity of the ancient Greek mind. Its appearance in a barbarian shrine in the foggy

Was Stonehenge an Ancient Observatory?

Of all the megalithic monuments, Stonehenge is without doubt the most popular—and the most highly publicized. In recent years, many speculative books and articles have been written about it, not only by archaeologists but also by astronomers and mathematicians; one best-selling book was the result of a computer analysis of Stonehenge. Some of the theories claiming that prehistoric men used Stonehenge as an observatory are summed up at right, accompanied by a schematized drawing that brings together all of the monument's elements from its various periods of development. The column of text, keyed by colour to the reconstruction, lists the archaeological and astronomical facts that seem to support the observatory theory.

Stonehenge as it appears today presents the outline of what could have been an observatory. Its remaining stones, concentrated at the monument's centre, represent roughly half of the megaliths that stood here at various stages of Stonehenge's development (c. 2750 B.C. to 1500 B.C.). In addition, various earthworks such as the bank, the ditch and rings of holes have since eroded or silted over. The axis of Stonehenge (arrow to top) is laid out so that it coincides with the direction of the sunrise on the day of the summer solstice.

The monument's entrance is at the top. At the entrance there are some 40 postholes (*small black dots*), which may have been used as markers of successive midwinter full-moon risings over a series of 18.6-year cycles. Astronomers know that such records can help in predicting eclipses.

There are 56 Aubrey Holes around the outside of the monument; the difference between five solar years and five lunar years is precisely 56 days. (Five solar years of 365.2 days each=1,826 days; five lunar years, each of 12 months of 29.5 days=1,770 days.)

The four Station Stones—black dots amid the Aubrey Holes—form a nearly perfect rectangle. The short sides of the rectangle point in the direction of the sunrise on the day of the summer solstice, while the long sides are aligned in the direction of the rising of the full moon nearest in time to the summer solstice. Significantly, Stonehenge is on the one latitude in the northern hemisphere where these two siting lines cross at right angles. Proponents of the observatory theory argue that the monument builders would not have dragged their huge stones for 20 miles unless they had realized that this site had a particular astronomical significance.

Inside the Aubrey Circle lie the two smaller rings of Y and Z holes. Since there are 29.5 days in the lunar month, the 59 holes in this combination of rings may have served as counters for two lunar months. By moving an indicator one hole each day, observers could count the passage of days in two lunar months.

The sarsen stones, forming the once-continuous ring of arches, were originally 30 in number. One of these stones (*lower right*) is markedly smaller than the 29 others. Theorists suggest that it represents a half day in the 29.5 lunar month.

Originally the Bluestone Circle probably contained 59 megaliths—once again, the total number of days in two lunar months.

The 19 bluestones that formed a horseshoe in the very centre of Stonehenge may have represented either the 19-year cycle or the 18.6-year cycle of the moon. Both cycles are important for the prediction of eclipses.

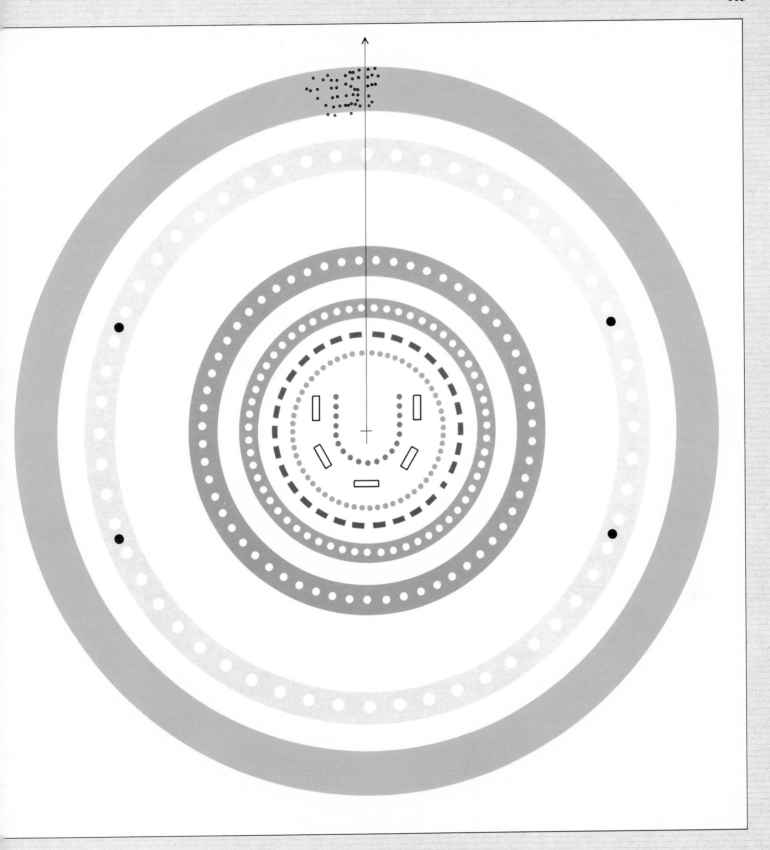

north, hundreds of years before any Greeks even existed, is a startling reminder that these were barbarians with considerable ingenuity of their own.

How far their ingenuity went has been the subject of much speculation, some of it highly imaginative. Some historians have examined Stonehenge and other megaliths with an eye and yardstick of faith and claim to have found measurements and relationships of extraordinary complexity and profound significance. These measurements, like similar ones of the Great Pyramid in Egypt, the temples of Akbar in India, Chartres Cathedral in France and the Pyramid of the Sun at Teotihuacán in Mexico, are said to spell out certain esoteric formulas that express the hidden harmonies of the heavens, the flow of the earth's magnetic currents, the pattern of past and future. By circumscribing the ground plans of the megaliths with triangles, pentagons and hexagons, and by measuring the distances between points on these figures and multiplying them or by finding their square roots, learned men have made calculations that they believe can be used to answer even such questions as the date of the Second Coming of Christ.

One book that provides some of the more extravagant theories is *The View over Atlantis*. Its author, John Michell, furnishes charts and plans demonstrating to his satisfaction that Stonehenge was "laid out according to the geometry and numbers of the Square of the Sun, and it contains its own hidden geometry, a pattern of energy that spirals away from the centre to spread over the surrounding countryside". This mystical Square of the Sun, Michell explains, is an arrangement of numbers in rows like those on a bingo card in which every row—vertical, horizontal or diagonal—adds up to 111, and the total sum of the numbers is 666, a figure rich in connotations for occultists and numerologists. Michell and his followers believe that it represents a concentration of divine wisdom, and therefore they view Stonehenge as a model of the New Jerusalem, the heavenly city that will be revealed on Judgment Day.

Most academic scholars dismiss this kind of speculation as nonsense. Yet recently, reputable scientists have begun to wonder if some megaliths were not, after all, designed to transmit, or at least represent, certain spiritual or learned traditions.

One who approached the mystery of the megaliths from a scientific viewpoint was Professor Gerald Hawkins of Boston University. In the 1960s he brought to the problem of Stonehenge not only a trained astronomer's eye but the services of a computer. Although he had visited Stonehenge, his measurements, observations and computations were made in Boston rather than at the site itself. They convinced him that Stonehenge had been an observatory of an exceedingly complex kind. According to Hawkins' findings, 18 lines of sight, through or across various standing stones, pointed to the rising or the setting of the sun or moon both in midsummer and midwinter with a margin of error so slight that the possibility of the stones being in chance alignments was only one in a couple of million.

Hawkins concluded that the builders of Stonehenge I had extensive astronomical knowledge (in fact, he believes that they used the Aubrey Holes to predict eclipses). But their methods were fairly crude; they erected only three stones. And what mainly interested them, Hawkins felt, was to stand at a certain spot and, looking over one of the stones, see some heavenly phenomenon occur on schedule. It was the builders of Stonehenge II and III who presumably made enormous strides in knowledge as well as in their sense of the dramatic, setting up the rest of the great stones with the certainty that heavenly bodies would appear precisely when predicted in the narrow slits between the boulders.

The results of Hawkins' work were summed up in his book *Stonehenge Decoded*. The book attracted a wide popular audience, but Hawkins' measurements and calculations drew sharp criticism from many archaeologists. They claimed that he made several fundamental calculating errors. In the first place, he based his computerized measurements on one plan that was obsolete and on another with only approximate measurements, intended merely to illustrate the general layout of Stonehenge. In the second place, Hawkins' critics maintained, he assumed that some of the stones shown on the plans as fallen or no longer existing had once stood in perfect alignment. That may not have been the case; and of course an error of even a centimetre would have been magnified to millions of miles in calculating angles out into the heavens. Still, although Hawkins' original calculations are rejected by many archaeologists, he is respected as an astronomer and has continued to study megalithic sites throughout the world. There is now considerable agreement with his theory that Stonehenge was indeed connected in some way with astronomical observations.

Alexander Thom, an Emeritus Professor of Engineering Science at Oxford University, has applied scientific theory to the megaliths to an even greater degree, and with characteristic Scottish practicality. He personally surveyed more than 600 standing stone megalithic sites in the British Isles, as well as the stone alignments at Carnac in Brittany. Thom not only is convinced that all of these structures were astronomic observatories of rare precision but that they were constructed according to a standard unit of measure, something that other investigators have long suspected. He calls this unit the megalithic yard. It measures 2.72 feet, a minute fraction less than the traditional Spanish vara, or rod, which Thom believes may itself be a survival from prehistory. He discovered that almost all the principal measurements —distances between stones, the circumference of circles, etc.—at many different monuments are multiples of 2.72 feet, suggesting that the megalith builders must have had yardsticks of this length, perhaps notched tree branches that they carefully preserved and transported to the new site for each construction project.

One of Thom's most interesting discoveries was that the builders avoided complex fractions wherever possible and tried to measure their principal lines in whole numbers of megalithic yards, often round numbers like 20 or 40. This naturally made for great difficulties when it came to laying out their circular monuments, since it is an axiom of geometry that you cannot have a whole number for both the diameter and the circumference of a circle. The megalith builders accordingly flattened their circles slightly or elongated them into ovoids and ellipses in order to get a circumference that could be expressed in a whole number of megalithic yards (*pages 110-111*). Some of their geometrical solutions to this and other complex problems Thom finds so intricate and so ingenious that a mathematician today would need a digital computer to work them out.

While Thom's analyses and conclusions, based on painstaking, firsthand observations, are not universally accepted by his colleagues, they have been less harshly criticized than Hawkins', and they have caused archaeologists to re-examine many of the sites Thom has measured. Even if Thom's conclusions are only partly valid, they indicate that the masters who designed many of the megaliths possessed great theoretical as well as practical knowledge.

These wise men may have made up a special caste of priests or seer-architects who enjoyed the respect and reverence of their people, and who willingly undertook long and tedious labours for them. Like the master builders of later times, these men probably would have been heirs to a body of more or less secret knowledge, passed down from generation to generation. Since writing would not come to Europe for many centuries, it would have been oral knowledge, made all the more impressive for having been committed to memory. Because the knowledge ap-

plied not only to building techniques but also to the passage of the heavenly bodies and the rotation of the seasons, it might have seemed even supernatural and would certainly have given its possessors enormous prestige among the simple folk.

No one can say if they turned this prestige to their own advantage by establishing a hereditary priesthood that exacted tithes or other practical expressions of faith. It is only in their rôle as architects that they can be perceived through the mists of the past. As creators of Europe's first monuments to be admired, and perhaps revered, they established a style unlike any that has succeeded them. Their megaliths seem to have no concern with grace or comfort, for they are not built to human scale. They are massive, solemn, brooding and as mysterious as the designs that cover some of their stones. Yet their anonymous builders, raising their great uncouth shapes in the wilderness, surely rank among the pioneers of human creative achievement.

The Epic Task of Building Stonehenge

Surveyors use a hide-rope compass to plot the perimeter of Stonehenge. Near by stands the Heel Stone, the site's first megalith.

One day nearly 4,000 years ago—it was probably spring—a group of families gathered on a rise on England's Salisbury Plain and started to draw a huge circle. Twelve hundred years and 40 generations would pass before their project would be finished.

Modern archaeologists now call the awesome result by the name of Stonehenge, and they have studied it so extensively that its construction can be illustrated in the detailed drawings on these pages. The birth of Stonehenge was that circle-scribing scene, which is shown above.

Moving over the soft turf, surveyors described the great outer circle by means of a colossal compass, a 160-foot length of oxhide rope affixed to a wooden peg at the circle's centre. As they etched its perimeter with a pointed stake fastened to the rope's outer end, men followed with measuring rods to check on the compass, for constant pulling could stretch the rope. The site was now ready for construction to begin.

Digging the Outermost Border

To form an enclosure for the stone structures they planned, the architects of Stonehenge constructed a pair of banks as the great outer circle. The method was simple but backbreaking; a trench was dug and the debris piled up on either side, forming a ridge about six feet high on the inner side (*above*) and a lower ridge on the outer side. The ditch-digging procedure was further complicated by the fact that beneath the cushiony sod lay solid chalk. Most able-bodied members of the community lent a hand in this project, the men excavating the hard ground with wooden digging sticks and antler picks, the women piling the loosened chalk into baskets. As these were then handed up to workers to dump on the parallel ridges, the great ditch-and-mound border slowly encircled Stonehenge's site.

Shaping the Sarsens to Proportion

To find structural material for their great trilithons, the builders of Stonehenge searched out mammoth boulders of sarsen—a variety of sandstone—in roughly rectangular shapes. The fact that sarsen was hard and naturally irregular proved no deterrent to builders with a firm purpose.

Crews of stone workers hiked some 20 miles cross country to Marlborough Downs, where sarsens were plentiful, measured blocks according to the planners' specifications and then set about fashioning them—using only simple stone mauls, fire, water and infinite patience to assist them.

Six men measure a flat-topped boulder of sarsen before cutting it to size. Each measuring stick, made of wood, is two megalithic yards long—just under five and a half feet. Charcoal is used for marking lines in the stone.

Twigs soaked in animal fat are laid along the precise line where the boulder is to be split. When the narrow strip is set afire, the stone beneath will expand slightly. One man fans the smouldering fire with a sheet of leather.

After the fire is doused and the embers brushed aside, one man pours cold water over the hot strip. Such cooling causes the stone to contract and split open. Other workers stand ready with stone mauls to pound in unison.

Hauling the Boulders Overland to the Site

At least 1,000 burly men were needed to transport a single sarsen stone to Stonehenge. To move a 50-ton sarsen over the hilly countryside, the workers built a sledge of square-cut timbers, and the monster slab was lashed onto it. Miles of vegetable-fibre rope were used in the operation—for holding the sledge together, for firmly fastening the sarsen to it and for the actual task of hauling the giant stone to its destination.

Once the stone was secure on the sledge, the whole rig was set on top of a series of oak rollers carved from tree trunks. As a sturdy crew inched the sledge slowly forwards, others quickly removed the rear rollers and carried them to the front, ready to receive the oncoming sledge.

Slowly the men traversed 20 miles of rough terrain. Easing the giant stone downhill was as arduous as inching it up the slopes. The human train, straining backwards on ropes to brake the downhill momentum of the burdened sledge, stretched even farther than the eye could see.

Levering the Upright into Position

Installing these sarsens required less manpower—but far more ingenuity —than transporting them. For each mammoth slab a deep, rectangular hole was dug, with three straight sides and the fourth sloping; the straight side across from the sloping one was shored up with stakes. Each sarsen, its bottom chipped to a blunt point, was brought in horizontal position (*below*) on rollers to the brink of the hole's sloping side. Slowly it was manœuvred down this side into the hole.

To raise it to vertical position, workers used a tower of crossed logs (*right*) as a fulcrum for long wooden levers that pried the sarsen upwards. By tugging downwards on the ropes tied to the levers' outer ends, the men painstakingly elevated the sarsen until it stood upright in its place.

Topping the Sarsens with their Lintels

The crowning glory of Stonehenge, the seven-ton lintels topping the sarsens, required less brute labour to set in place than inventiveness and persistence. But it was a perilous task, because one slip could mean disaster.

Before the workers raised each lintel, they smoothed its surface with stone mauls (*below, right*). That step finished, they rolled the lintel to the position on the ground parallel to where it would be set on two uprights.

Next the men pried the stone off the ground with levers, first a few inches at one end, then a few at the other, with logs shoved under the raised ends. The process was repeated and logs piled up under each end until the stone was about six feet off the ground. A crew built a crib of logs alongside raised stones and nudged it over to rest on top of the crib. The prying and propping up of the ends of the stone were repeated until the lintel was level with the tops of the two uprights. Gently, the stone slid sideways until it lay perched, 13 feet in the air, on top of its sarsen uprights.

Chapter Six: The Fall of the Megaliths

For years conjecture and controversy have swirled around the question: why did men start to put up megaliths in the first place? Less attention has been paid to the equally intriguing and puzzling question: why did the builders stop? Here was a form of communal expression, a style of architecture and of life that flourished for 3,000 years. This is a span of cultural unity unmatched at any time in history—longer than the Old Kingdom of Egypt or any dynasty of China—and it involved a vigorous people who were constantly expanding their geographical and technological horizons.

The archaeological record shows no sign of a violent break in their lives, no sudden change of climate, no volcanic catastrophe, no tidal waves. The level of material life, of agricultural and metallurgical techniques seems to have gone on rising steadily century by century. Transportation became easier with the cutting of the forests; the wheel and the smithy spread across Europe; trade accelerated and so did the diffusion of products and ideas.

Up through the middle of the Second Millennium B.C. the great works went on: new monuments were raised and old ones were redesigned. Gradually, however, the pace of building slowed down. Then, around 1500 B.C., after the construction of a group of about 50 small tombs on the Isles of Scilly, off the southwest coast of England, megalith building came to an end. No more did men move colossal stones across

Labelled "An Abury Atto de fe", this drawing by antiquarian William Stukeley was an early plea for the protection of archaeological finds. It shows the megalithic site of Avebury being systematically destroyed by sledge hammers and fires —a practice, Stukeley indignantly wrote, that greedy farmers and builders fervently engaged in "for a little dirty profit".

the moors and streams; no more did they arrange those stones to track new astronomical observations or to reflect changes in their religion. A whole dimension faded from the life of Europe, and only a few explanations—and tentative ones at that—can be offered to account for its disappearance.

Perhaps men stopped building megaliths because of the increasing insecurity of life in the later Bronze Age and even more in the subsequent Iron Age. Neolithic communities, widely separated by stretches of forest, had been able to live at peace without worrying about hostile incursions, except from occasional gangs of brigands. But once men began to organize themselves in larger groups equipped with new weapons, first of bronze, later of iron, they could lay waste whole communities. From now on these communities would focus their efforts not on works of peace like Stonehenge but on defences against encroachment. Fortified camps and towns are characteristic structures of postmegalithic times.

Bronze and iron provided not only weapons but new tools, and so men were now doing other things as well; they were engaging, for example, in a more intensive and more settled kind of agriculture. Farmers occupied with cultivating fields and caring for livestock had little time to construct megaliths. As wealth grew and trade increased with central Europe and the Mediterranean, labour became more specialized and social classes began to stratify. Having learned how to master animals, men of the Bronze Age learned how to master one another. Warrior aristocrats discovered they could persuade peasants and herdsmen to provide them with the wherewithal for a life of feasting and fighting. In the Bronze and Iron Age societies described in the Homeric poems and in old Irish legends, a boastful and quarrelsome upper class spends most of its time picking fights with its neighbours while an amorphous class of serfs tends the livestock and brews the beer. In such a society individual achievements would command attention, and the inclination would be—and was—to put up rich memorials to single heroes rather than the anonymous collective monuments of the old days.

Population changes, the result of one group coming in to overwhelm or dominate or simply influence another, may also have played a part. The evidence of skeletons indicates that the population of Western Europe was fairly homogeneous and stable all through the Neolithic Age. But as the age of metal begins, the picture becomes clouded by newcomers of obscure origins. The Beaker People, wherever they came from (*Chapter 3*), had different practices from those of the neolithic farmers; they introduced single-grave burial to Britain, for one thing. They also may have had different beliefs that resulted in some changes in the old megalithic building style.

More or less contemporary with the Beakers were the Battle-Axe, or Corded-Ware, People, named after weapons and patterned pottery they buried with their dead. Excavations in the Netherlands have brought to light possible clues to their origins: a model of a two-wheeled chariot and solid wooden wheels somewhat similar to those used slightly before this time —the middle of the Third Millennium—on carts in the Russian steppes. From such admittedly flimsy evidence, some archaeologists have deduced that the Battle-Axe People came from the East. If they had carts, they may also have had horses; in any event, they were mobile. That, together with their finely polished weapons, would have given them a terrifying advantage over small, static farming communities. With their superior techniques of war, the Battle-Axe People could have overrun vast reaches with only a few men, as Cortes was to destroy the mighty neolithic empire of Mexico with a small force of cavalry.

Not all scholars are convinced that the Battle-Axe People were invaders; some argue that the axes and wheels credited to them may have been evolved by previous local cultures. In any event, most of the continent bears witness to settlement, between the 15th and Eighth centuries B.C., by several later peoples who cremated their dead and buried urns of their ashes in cemeteries. Together these peoples form the so-called Urnfield Cultures. But whether they imposed themselves on Europe by conquest or trickled in by migration is not known; the ashes in the urns tell no tales about the life of flesh and bone.

Only one invasion in neolithic times can be clearly documented, and that occurred on the island of Corsica, far from the principal megalithic sites. Here the French archaeologist Roger Grosjean has recently studied a group of menhirs that dramatically reflect a time of great troubles.

Corsica had been inhabited for centuries by a peaceful people who herded sheep and goats, wore wool garments, built megalithic tombs and carved human features in upright slabs that were from six to 10 feet high. They led a quiet life until a sea incursion by a fierce group of raiders late in the Second Millennium B.C. The invaders, whom Grosjean calls Torreans because they built round stone towers known in the local dialect as *torre*, carried long bronze swords that were far superior to anything in the Corsican armament. When not engaged in martial adventures, they bred cattle, fashioned leather clothes and followed a cult the deified the bull. Their way of life differed totally from that of the native Corsicans, and there was apparently no meeting ground between the two groups. The Torreans, who never represented the human figure in art, knocked down the statue-menhirs they found and added insult by using fragments of the statues to construct walls. The inhabitants, driven from their fertile lowland fields to the barren uplands, looked down with fear and envy on the swaggering invaders below. Possibly to bewitch their conquerors, they set up statue-menhirs with unmistakably Torrean hallmarks, notably the long swords the Torreans hung around their necks. At the sides of the heads of these figures are round holes that must have held horns, perhaps similar to the horns on Torrean helmets.

This Corsican episode by itself would be curious enough, but there may be more to it. At Medinet Habu in Egypt, a thousand miles across the Mediterranean from Corsica, there is a famous bas-relief commemorating the victory of Ramses III in the year 1190 B.C. over an invading horde of pirates called the Peoples of the Sea. On the inscription accompanying the bas-relief some of these peoples are identified as Shardana (which sounds like Sardinia, the island south of Corsica), and on the relief they are wearing horned helmets and carrying long bronze swords. Grosjean suggests that these Shardana, or a related group, went marauding elsewhere in the western Mediterranean, either before or after their repulse by Ramses, and that they found and destroyed the megalithic culture on Corsica.

If there were similar assaults on megalithic cultures on the European continent, no bas-reliefs record them. The light of history breaks on northern and Western Europe only with the arrival in about 500 B.C. of Greek traders and colonists. By then most of what had been the megalithic region was lorded over by a proto-Celtic-speaking people who seem to have arrived in several waves from central Europe, beginning as early as 800 B.C., and to have taken over control of the older populations. The Celts themselves were turbulent and individualistic. They coated their hair with limewash; they had iron swords and fought from chariots. Their fervid imaginations filled the megalithic burial mounds with the ghosts of gods and heroes they had overcome. The Celts were not a people to band together in peace and indulge in the long slow work of erecting megaliths; their efforts at construction were devoted to hill-forts to protect themselves from one another.

In the long run, neither war nor social change nor population change adequately explains why the monument builders halted their labours, and in the present state of knowledge it is idle to expect to find any single and simple answer. No doubt the simplest answer is the best one: there are moments in history when any culture, having endured for centuries and given every outward sign of health and prosperity almost up to the very end, lives itself out. Of course, it could have been some sudden development. In the Seventh Century A.D. a few troops of horsemen, sweeping out of Arabia like a hot desert wind, overwhelmed the rich old Greco-Roman civilization of Syria and North Africa; the same may have happened to the megalithic culture of Western Europe. But except for the Torreans of Corsica, there is no sure clue to indicate that it did.

When the megalith building finally ceased, around

1500 B.C., Western Europe must have abounded in monuments old and new, tens of thousands of them, most of them intact and dominating the landscape with their bulk. And the traditions associated with them would have been very much alive, for nothing that had so long absorbed the physical and spiritual energies of so many people could vanish overnight; instead, the uses to which the monuments had been put gradually changed. Many of the megaliths retained their aura of sanctity. Many were still used as graves and some as shrines, but others came to serve as campsites or degenerated into garbage dumps. Some were turned into fortified castles of the new aristocracy, which seems to have happened to some of the passage-grave mounds in Ireland; others were taken over by alien priesthoods for the practice of their rites. But many, despite the new priests' repeated objections, continued to be used by the peasant folk who lived around them for primordial rituals that they scarcely understood.

Of all the priesthoods associated with the megaliths, the most famous are the Druids—who not only served the Celts of France and Britain but may also have made their laws. It has been an article of popular belief that Druids built the megaliths. They did not appear, however, until the First Century B.C., and

Man's changing beliefs are reflected in this 25-foot-tall menhir at Saint-Duzec in Brittany. The monument, originally stark and unadorned, was erected by Stone Age residents of Brittany in the Third Millennium B.C. With the Christian Era, churchmen sought to replace the stone's pagan associations with Christian ones. Near the end of the 17th Century a cross was installed, and the section below it was carved with representations of the instruments associated with the Passion of Christ, including a ladder and a lance. The painting of the Crucifixion was added later, and has often been retouched because Brittany's moisture erodes the pigments.

it is not even certain that they used stone structures for their religious rites. In the writings of Julius Caesar and other Romans, the Druids are reported to hold their services in oak groves, and no mention is made of temples. These writers, of course, frequently got their information second-hand and may not have known what they were talking about, since Druid rites were carefully shielded from foreigners. There would seem to be no reason why the Druids should not have taken over the megaliths, as the Christians took over the Pantheon in Rome from the pagans and made it a church and as the Turks took over the church of Saint Sophia in Istanbul from the Christians and made it a mosque.

Apart from some Iron Age pottery found at Stonehenge that may or may not have been of Druid making, there is no physical trace of their occupancy of the megalithic sites until long afterwards, in the late 18th Century, when the cult was either revived —or re-created—by the Welsh antiquarian Iolo Morganwg. Bands of Druids, or pseudo-Druids, still exist; in 1966 Dr. Thomas Maughan, who calls himself the reincarnated Chief Druid of the British Circle of the Universal Bond, talked the British government into letting his disciples take over Stonehenge every Midsummer Eve for their dances and ululations, to the amusement of sceptical tourists and the annoyance of orthodox archaeologists.

If the real Druids did not actually make use of megalithic sites, there is evidence that the Romans, who suppressed the Druids' bloody rituals and political independence, occupied some of the monuments. At Dorchester in England, they made an amphitheatre of the conveniently circular ancient henge monument. In France, in the region around Paris, they left Gallo-Roman pottery in many megalithic tombs. In the village of Ploufragan in Brittany, a wealthy family of the Roman period used one compartment of a gallery grave as living quarters. Gold coins with effigies of imperial Romans have been dug up around Stonehenge.

Coins are artifacts to be considered warily. Because they bear dates, they are tempting to the seeker of facts. But they were also easily carried far afield. Roman coins have been found around the Boyne graves in Ireland, a country the Roman legions never touched. Such currency may have crossed the seas in commerce between Britannia and Hibernia; it may have been brought there by Roman tourists who, like Pliny the Elder, were always ready to travel to inspect some natural or human wonder. Most of the coins found at Stonehenge, however, date to the dark days of the Fourth Century, when civilized Europe was on the brink of barbarian domination and chaos.

Perhaps the crisis brought the native Britons—who were never fully Romanized—to worship at the ancient shrine. Even if it were in ruins, even if the very name of the divinity who had presided over its construction had long been forgotten, what could have been more reassuring of stability than old Stonehenge? While savage Saxons ravaged the land and burned the cities and suburban villas built by the Romans, the ancient and durable stones of Stonehenge would have offered a symbolic promise of continuing survival.

The Romans were not the only authority to find the stones a persisting influence on the peoples' minds; so did the Christian church. Its repeated fulminations against assorted practices connected with the monuments indicate how deeply ingrained and hard they were to extirpate. A Sixth Century Spanish bishop denounced the "worship of the devil" that was being carried on in the form of "lighting candles at stones"—very likely megaliths. The Council of Nantes in 658 directed "bishops and their servants to dig up and remove and hide in places where they cannot be found, those stones which in remote and woody places are still worshipped and where vows are made". Church councils at Arles in 452, at Tours in 567, at Toledo in 681 also issued edicts against the worship of stones. Kings as well as churchmen denounced the stones; there are injunctions against them in the laws of Charlemagne in Eighth Century France, of Alfred the Great in Ninth Century Wessex, of Canute the Great in 11th Century England and Scandinavia.

In the Middle Ages megalith wrecking itself became a superstitious rite. At Avebury in southern England, the local residents mutilated and cast down one of the giant stones every 25 years to symbolize the exorcising of the devil. During one of these ceremonies a barber-surgeon was crushed when a stone toppled before he could get out of its way. Since the engineering resources of a 14th Century village were insufficient to raise so many tons, he was buried where he lay, and there his bones were found some centuries later, with his scissors lying alongside him and a pouch containing coins dating to the reign of King Edward I. That middle-class citizens took part in a project requiring such manual labour shows how well the Church had succeeded in its megalith-destroying campaign, making the task as much a communal effort as megalith building had been in the first place.

If obliterating the monuments was not always feasible, there was another way of dealing with them, and that was to Christianize them. A 12th Century account of the life of Saint Samson—one of the most reliable biographies of the Celtic saints—records how that holy man found people on a hillside in Cornwall worshipping "an abominable image". He performed a miracle on the spot, converting and baptizing the people. "On this hill I myself have been", says his biographer, "and with my own hands have traced the sign of the cross which Saint Samson with his own hands carved by means of an iron instrument on a standing stone".

Similar transformations occurred elsewhere in the British Isles and on the Continent. In Brittany many menhirs have had crosses erected on top of them (*page 134*) and other Christian symbols placed on them. At Yspytty Cynfyn in Wales, megaliths serve as the partial boundary of a circular churchyard. Twenty miles away, the pulpit of the church at Llanfairpwllgwyngyll is built directly above a menhir. In two small Portuguese churches and at a chapel in northern Brittany, megalithic chamber tombs serve as side chapels. At Gangas de Onis in northern Spain, a Romanesque church of the 10th and 11th centuries is built on a mound over a passage grave; the capstone of the grave is the church altar stone.

The original megalithic monuments are not always visible in the renovations made by later peoples. The site of the Mound of Hostages at Tara, in Ireland, is an example. Tara was the spiritual centre of ancient Ireland. Saint Patrick went there to debate with the Druid Lucetmael—a decisive episode in Irish history and one that James Joyce utilized in *Finnegans Wake*. In the 1950s, Pro-

Although it looks like a battered army bunker, this stone structure is a 55-foot gallery grave known as La Pierre Folle, or The Crazy Stone. The family in whose farmyard it was discovered used its cavernous chamber as a hen house and a storeroom for farm implements. Today it is considered one of the finest megalithic relics in western France.

Not far from La Pierre Folle, on the river Vienne, this bizarre, megalith-crowned Christian chapel, called La Chapelle Dolmen, stands out in the underbrush like a top-heavy temple. The three-and-a-half-foot-thick megalithic capstone's original supports were replaced in the 11th Century by these four delicate Romanesque columns.

fessor Sean P. O. Ríordáin dug into the Mound of Hostages and found a Bronze Age passage grave. More digging uncovered some later secondary burials. Clearly, Tara had been an important shrine before there was ever a king or a Christian saint in Ireland. Further excavation will surely reveal many more such sites throughout Europe.

The megaliths have suffered not only the rage of the righteous, but also the depredations of grave robbers. (Even Saint Patrick, according to the old Irish book *The Colloquy of the Ancients*, robbed megalithic tombs, no doubt in the hope of breaking the superstitious hold they had on his flock.) The robbers were drawn by the fact that princely burials had taken place at many of the tombs. The difficulty of moving the immense stones that sealed the tombs lent a superstitious dread to the plunderers' work; it was easy to suppose that supernatural forces protected the tombs against profane hands. This belief is reflected in literature. In the Eighth Century Anglo-Saxon epic *Beowulf*, describing events of some 300 years earlier, a fire-breathing dragon guards a treasure in a barrow by the sea. When a robber steals some gold from it, the dragon sets all of King Beowulf's country aflame. The aged hero meets his death killing the dragon:

> *The wise old warrior sank down by the wall*
> *And stared at the work of the giants of old,*
> *The arches of stone and the standing columns*
> *Upholding the ancient earth-hall within.*

The "work of the giants of old" clearly refers to a megalithic grave.

A later opus, a Norse saga, recounts the impact of a Viking break-in at Maes Howe, a megalithic site in the Orkneys. The Vikings, who were on their way to a crusade, actually made two break-ins there in the 1150s. At the second, the warriors had barely landed when, says the saga, "a snow storm drove over them, and there two men of their band lost their wits, and that was a great hindrance to their journey". The dragon, it would seem, was still guarding its hoard. The Vikings left many scratchings on the walls at Maes Howe, including drawings of a dragon and a walrus, 14 signatures and many runic verses. One of the latter records:

> *A long time ago was a great treasure hidden here.*
> *Lucky will he be who can find the great fortune.*
> *Häkon single-handed bore treasure from this howe.*

The ordinary people who lived near the megaliths proved even more destructive than the grave robbers and the Christian prelates together. The monuments were, in effect, ready-made quarries, providing handy building blocks for houses and pig pens; rock pillars were regularly chipped and battered to furnish gravel for roads. Many a charming rural village like Avebury is built largely of fragments of the great stone shrine in whose shadow it grew. In Brittany and other regions with stony soil the earthen mounds covering the tombs were scratched off by peasants seeking to enrich their own thin plots.

And along with the human depredators, the natural forces of rain and wind and frost, lightning and flood were at work. Stones fell over; others cracked and were split apart by roots working their way into the cracks. Mounds were worn down. Grass grew where there had been chalk surfaces. Ground that had been beaten flat by the feet of thousands of pilgrims relapsed to wilderness.

In an 1836 sketch, two antiquarians, Alexander Blair and Francis Ronalds, engage in the gentlemanly pastime of measuring a menhir at Carnac. Interest in the megaliths ran high among the well-to-do in 19th Century France and England, but scientific accuracy seldom resulted from their efforts.

However the stones themselves fared, the knowledge about them and the rituals that surrounded them remained alive in the form of local superstitions. The French poet Denis Roche, in *Carnac*, a book published in 1969, calls a roll of megalithic sites in Brittany and cites a number of ritual practices performed upon or around them down to recent times. At Locronon sterile women sat on a shapeless rock called the Stone Mare in the hope of becoming fertile. At Crozon girls about to be wed sat astride the menhir for the same purpose. At Saint-Enéour, on the second Sunday of September, girls danced around the menhir called the Stone Mast, which is in the square in front of the village church, to assure themselves husbands and children. At Lesmon girls slid down the menhir on their bare bottoms—again for the same purpose. A variation occurred at Carnac, at the menhir called Le Vaisseau; by the light of the full moon, young married couples stripped naked and chased around the stone while their parents kept watch from the top of another menhir. Apparently the neolithic fertility goddess never quite lost her sway in Brittany.

Neolithic rituals also lingered elsewhere. Until about 1870 in County Clare in Ireland, an annual fair used to be held near a barrow in a lonely spot, with foot races run alongside the mound. A few years after the last fair, when a road contractor demolished the mound for its limestone chips, a megalithic tomb was uncovered. Perhaps funeral games and races had been held on that very spot when the first bodies were entombed there; perhaps the festivities had gone on year after year down through time, long after the tomb itself was only a clouded memory in the minds of the local peasantry. However that may be, it is very likely that the fair was a persistent echo of

This 1805 drawing of the aligned stones at Carnac shows how large the megaliths loomed in 19th Century imaginations: they appear as a veritab

forest some 30 or 40 feet high, dwarfing the men who are surveying them. In reality, the stones are four to 14 feet high and much farther apart.

the reverence that had once been given to bones and stones. It is significant that all these rituals surrounding the monuments were the rituals of country people, the pagans par excellence—*pagani* was the Latin word meaning country people.

With the beginning of modern times, the megaliths —earlier at the mercy of the Church, the kings, the robbers, the squatters and the weather—faced a new threat in the form of scientific progress. The 18th and 19th centuries brought radical changes—in agriculture, in construction and in travel. For people interested in improving their acres, megaliths were annoyances sitting in the middle of fields, taking up good cropland. The ancestors of these people may have grumbled at running into a 40-ton boulder, but not being able to do much about it, they ploughed around it. The later generations of farmers had the equipment, the energy and the know-how to destroy the rocks—and to make a little money on the side by selling them for fill and road material. They attacked the stones with enthusiasm.

In 1743 Dr. William Stukeley, a pioneer in field archaeology, recorded the scene in England with some anguish: "The barbarous massacre of a stone here with leavers and hammers, sledges and fires, is as terrible a sight as a Spanish Atto de fe. The vast cave they dig around it, the hollow under the stone like a glass-house furnace or a baker's oven, the huge chasms made through the body of the stone, the straw, the faggots, the smoak, the prongs, and squallor of the fellows looks like a knot of devils grilling the soul of a sinner."

Wealthy collectors found that megaliths fitted in very nicely with their new notions of landscape gardening. In 1792 one of them, Lord Arundel, had a grotto built for his enjoyment at Wardour Castle in Wiltshire; three megalithic stones from a near-by tomb were carted off to be tastefully worked into the "very sheltered and gloomy" retreat.

In France a lady with a fancy for dolmens bought a megalithic tomb in Brittany for 100 francs and had it moved 250 miles to the town of Confolens. When she died she was sealed in a carved sarcophagus set on top of the capstone. A family named Piketti outdid her. They had a rectangular megalithic tomb moved from Brittany to the cemetery at Meudon outside Paris, where they had it fashioned into a family vault. Nine members of the family lie there, so it has a useful function, serving the purpose for which it was designed in the first place thousands of years ago —as a collective tomb.

What farming, engineering and landscaping left undamaged was dealt with in the new vogue for travel. In the 19th Century tourists cheerfully vandalized the megaliths, evincing no guilt. At Stonehenge a large mallet hung on a peg so visitors could chip souvenirs off the ancient sarsen stones. Only the extraordinary hardness of the stones preserved them from ending up as fragments in a million cottages.

But side by side with these destructive tendencies ran another current. Before the 18th Century ended, the megaliths began to attract the interest of antiquarians. And 19th Century romantics, enamoured of blood-stained ruins and other relics of the past, took naturally to the megaliths, "the phantom forms of antediluvian giants", as Sir Walter Scott called them. Turner and Constable and a host of lesser artists painted them in ominous shapes. The poet William Wordsworth in *The Prelude* evoked a megalithic "sacrificial altar, fed with living men—how deep the groans!" The heroine of Thomas Hardy's *Tess of the d'Urbervilles*, after killing the man who seduced her, flees to the "heathen temple" of Stonehenge and gives herself up to the police as the sun rises, flaming, over the "stone of sacrifice".

Artists and writers and antiquarians, as well as curiosity seekers of all sorts, clambered over the monuments for a century or more before there was any serious scientific investigation of the megaliths. There was not even a generic word for them until 1849, when the British antiquarian Algernon Herbert coined the word "megalith" in an odd book called *Cyclops Christianus: or, an Argument to Disprove the Supposed Antiquity of Stonehenge and other Megalithic Erections in England and Brittany*. As is evident in the title, his arguments did not hold up, but the name he gave to the tombs did. And the scholarly interest in the monuments continued. In 1872 came James Fergusson's *Rude Stone Monuments in All Countries: Their Age and Uses*. Fergusson mistakenly believed that the megaliths were "erected by partially civilized races after they had come into contact with the Romans", but his book is worthy of note because it is one of the earliest systematic studies of the megaliths. In 1876 the Swedish scholar Oscar Montelius made the first major attempt to classify the monuments, and suggested three categories of tomb types quite similar to the categories described in Chapter 1. From then on excavations, discoveries, theories and reconstructions came apace. One of the most important of the findings, of course, was that the great stone structures were much older than they had been thought to be.

Today interest in the monuments runs high. Even so, occasional depredations still occur. Contractors working for land developers have destroyed some megaliths that lay concealed in the ground, and a few people have gone on putting monuments to utilitarian purposes. The capstone of a megalithic chamber near Saumur served as a bridge across the Loire during the 19th Century, and a gallery grave in the Loire Valley serves as a farmer's outdoor oven.

Fortunately, the main trend these days is towards preservation. The megaliths are increasingly regarded as national treasures, indeed as treasures of all mankind, and efforts have been undertaken to protect them from further dilapidation and decay. Many fallen stones have been lifted and many ancient sites cleaned up and restored, though not always to the satisfaction of archaeological purists. Some stones have been removed to museums; many have wire fences around them. Sightseers now come up by busloads and file solemnly through Stonehenge and Carnac —but they wield cameras instead of the souvenir-chipping hammers of old.

What message do these latter-day pilgrims take away? What message can be read from these monuments that survive from a time when almost nothing we now take for granted in ordinary life yet existed?

The first overwhelming feeling that strikes most visitors to the megaliths is that there is no connection between them and life as we know it today. The stones are so old they are not only prehistoric, they belong to another kind of existence. They are gaunt reminders that a way of life can long flourish and then vanish, leaving behind nothing but mystery. Except for a few surviving local superstitions, there seems to be no link between these stupendous wrecks and contemporary life.

Yet there may be a connection after all. Suppose that the findings of such mathematicians as Alexander Thom, discussed in the previous chapter, are firmly established and generally accepted. We would then be compelled to conclude that an intense fire of learning flamed through Europe for many centuries, long before anyone dreamed that such learning existed. Could that fire have entirely sputtered out, leaving no trace? The answer to this question may lie in a look at some later history.

Since the days of Pythagoras, the Greek sage and mathematician of the Sixth Century B.C., Western man has been haunted from time to time by the idea that the key to the construction of the universe is really a harmony of numbers. It is an idea that entered reputable philosophy through Plato, and esoteric and magical literature through the cabalists. It also entered the craft of mediaeval builders in formulas and plans for the symmetry of their structures. It is an airy and sometimes foggy doctrine, often leading to great foolishness, but turning up in the strongholds of common sense and science as well. Modern thought and life have been profoundly influenced by Niels Bohr's planetary model of the atom and by the double-spiral model of the molecule DNA,

the chain of heredity, devised by Francis H. C. Crick and James D. Watson. Both these concepts can be described as Pythagorean abstractions.

Long ago, in the First Century A.D., Clement of Alexandria, one of the Church Fathers and a man of learning, recorded that Pythagoras derived his philosophy from the "Gauls and other barbarians". Another early tradition held that Pythagoras was a disciple of Abaris the Hyperborean, i.e., the Briton; still others say Pythagoras was inspired by the Indians, the Babylonians, the Egyptians or the god Hermes. There may be no particular reason to believe one of these versions over another; but the intriguing possibility exists that this idea of the mathematical harmony of nature—which has been one of the most persistent, most seminal, most maddening and most enlightening concepts in man's intellectual history—goes back to the monument builders. The possibility exists that our Bohrs and Cricks and Watsons, with their dreams of simple mathematical harmonies that underlie the complexities of cold fact, are the direct heirs of the wise old Stone Age men who spent their lives tracking the revolutions of the sun and the moon and working out ways to record them in everlasting stone.

A Timeless Monument of Many Moods

In the grey-blue light of dawn, the enormous megaliths of Stonehenge poke their roughhewn heads into a thin, slowly rising mist.

On the way to Stonehenge, today's traveller may think of the monument as a mystery solved, or about to be solved. He knows of recent speculation that Stonehenge was an astronomical observatory, and even though the theory is still unproved it seems only a matter of time before the ancient stones will yield up their secrets to modern scientific research. But then the traveller comes upon the great brooding mass, and his confidence is quickly shaken.

The crude beauty and power of Stonehenge is strangely disturbing. So too is the illusion of constantly changing shapes as light and shadow play on the weathered stones. The monument's remote location on an empty plain and its concentric rings of megaliths are obviously purposeful. They demand some kind of explanation. Yet despite all the fascinating conjecture, Stonehenge will probably remain a magnificent mystery—if only because it is the expression of an ancient, unfathomable mentality.

A 4,500-year-old enigma, Stonehenge stands in lofty repose, bathed in the pale afternoon light. This photograph, dominated by the towering forms

f two slab-roofed trilithons, was taken just outside the ponderous ring of sarsen stones, looking through the monument towards the southwest.

Rough-textured against a velvety late-afternoon sky, Stonehenge's megaliths cast long shadows in this view from the altar stone inside the inne

circle, facing northeast towards the Heel Stone (through arch, centre left). Like spokes in a giant wheel, the shadows rotate as the earth turns.

Transformed by dusk, the concentric rings of Stonehenge appear to stretch out in a straight line, and the megaliths' bulky shapes are converted

into silhouettes cut from black paper. Minutes after this picture was taken, the illusion changed as the monument swallowed up the setting sun.

The monumental size of Stonehenge is emphasized as the full moon rides high to the southeast and hangs over an outlying bluestone framed by

...wo trilithons. If Stonehenge was indeed an observatory, this same view probably figured in lunar calculations made at least 4,500 years ago.

The Emergence of Man

This chart records the progression of life on earth from its first appearance in the warm waters of the new-formed planet through the evolution of man himself; it traces his physical, social, technological and intellectual development to the Christian era. To place these advances in commonly used chronological sequences, the column at the

Geology	Archaeology	Thousand Millions of Years Ago	
Precambrian earliest era		4.5	Creation of the Earth
		4	Formation of the primordial sea
		3	First life, single-celled algae and bacteria, appears in water
		2	
		1	

Geology	Archaeology	Millions of Years Ago	
			First oxygen-breathing animals appear
		800	
			Primitive organisms develop interdependent specialized cells
		600	Shell-bearing multicelled invertebrate animals appear
Palaeozoic ancient life			Evolution of armoured fish, first animals to possess backbones
		400	Small amphibians venture on to land
			Reptiles and insects arise
			Thecodont, ancestor of dinosaurs, arises
Mesozoic middle life		200	Age of dinosaurs begins
			Birds appear
			Mammals live in shadow of dinosaurs
			Age of dinosaurs ends
		80	
			Prosimians, earliest primates, develop in trees
Cainozoic recent life		60	
		40	Monkeys and apes evolve
		20	
		10	Ramapithecus, oldest known primate with apparently man-like traits, evolves in India and Africa
		8	
		6	
		4	Australopithecus, closest primate ancestor to man, appears in Africa

Geology	Archaeology	Millions of Years Ago	
Lower Pleistocene oldest period of most recent epoch	**Lower Palaeolithic** oldest period of Old Stone Age	2	Oldest known tool fashioned by man in Africa
		1	First true man, Homo erectus, emerges in East Indies and Africa
			Homo erectus populates temperate zone

Geology	Archaeology	Thousands of Years Ago	
Middle Pleistocene middle period of most recent epoch		800	Man learns to control and use fire
		600	
		400	Large-scale, organized elephant hunts staged in Europe
			Man begins to make artificial shelters from branches
		200	
Upper Pleistocene latest period of most recent epoch	**Middle Palaeolithic** middle period of Old Stone Age		Neanderthal man emerges in Europe
		80	
		60	Ritual burials in Europe and Middle East suggest belief in afterlife
			Woolly mammoths hunted by Neanderthal in northern Europe
		40	Cave bear becomes focus of cult in Europe
	Upper Palaeolithic latest period of Old Stone Age		Cro-Magnon man arises in Europe
			Asian hunters cross Bering Land Bridge to populate New World
			Oldest known written record, lunar notations on bone, made in Europe
			Man reaches Australia
			First artists decorate walls and ceilings of caves in France and Spain
		30	Figurines sculpted for nature worship
		20	Invention of needle makes sewing possible
			Bison hunting begins on Great Plains of North America
Holocene present epoch	**Mesolithic** Middle Stone Age	10	Bow and arrow invented in Europe
			Pottery first made in Japan

(Last Ice Age — spanning Upper Pleistocene / Middle and Upper Palaeolithic)

▼ Four thousand million years ago

▼ Three thousand million years ago

▲ Origin of the Earth (4,500 million)

▲ First life (3,500 million)

ar left of each of the chart's four sections identifies the great geoogical eras into which the earth's history is divided by scientists, hile the second column lists the archaeological ages of human hisory. The key dates in the rise of life and of man's outstanding accomplishments appear in the third column (years and events mentioned in this volume of The Emergence of Man appear in bold type). The chart is not to scale; the reason is made clear by the bar below, which represents in linear scale the 4,500 million years spanned by the chart—on the scaled bar, the portion relating to the total period of known human existence (*far right*) is too small to be distinguished.

Geology	Archaeology	Years B.C.	
Holocene *(cont.)*	Neolithic New Stone Age	9000	
			Sheep domesticated in Middle East
			Dog domesticated in North America
		8000	Jericho, oldest known city, settled
			Goat domesticated in Persia
			Man cultivates his first crops, wheat and barley, in Middle East
		7000	Pattern of village life grows in Middle East
			Catal Hüyük, in what is now Turkey, becomes largest Neolithic city
			Loom invented in Middle East
			Cattle domesticated in Middle East
		6000	Agriculture begins to replace hunting in Europe
	Copper Age		Copper used in trade in Mediterranean area
			Corn cultivated in Mexico
		4800	**Oldest known massive stone monument built in Brittany**
		4000	Sail-propelled boats used in Egypt
			First city-states develop in Sumer
			Cylinder seals begin to be used as marks of identification in Middle East
		3500	First potatoes grown in South America
			Wheel originates in Sumer
			Man begins to cultivate rice in Far East
			Silk moth domesticated in China
			Egyptian merchant trading ships start to ply the Mediterranean
			First writing, pictographic, composed in Middle East
	Bronze Age	3000	Bronze first used to make tools in Middle East
			City life spreads to Nile Valley
			Plough is developed in Middle East
			Accurate calendar based on stellar observation devised in Egypt
		2800	**Stonehenge, most famous of ancient stone monuments, begun in England**
			Pyramids built in Egypt
			Minoan navigators begin to venture into seas beyond the Mediterranean
		2600	Variety of gods and heroes glorified in *Gilgamesh* and other epics in Middle East

Geology	Archaeology	Years B.C.	
Holocene *(cont.)*	Bronze Age *(cont.)*	2500	Cities rise in the Indus Valley
			Earliest written code of laws drawn up in Sumer
			Herdsmen of Central Asia learn to tame and ride horses
		2000	Use of bronze in Europe
			Chicken and elephant domesticated in Indus Valley
			Eskimo culture begins in Bering Strait area
		1500	Invention of ocean-going outrigger canoes enables man to reach islands of South Pacific
			Ceremonial bronze sculptures created in China
			Imperial government, ruling distant provinces, established by Hittites
		1400	Iron in use in Middle East
			First complete alphabet devised in script of the Ugarit people in Syria
			Hebrews introduce concept of monotheism
	Iron Age	1000	Reindeer domesticated in Eurasia
		900	Phoenicians develop modern alphabet
		800	Use of iron begins to spread throughout Europe
			Nomads create a far-flung society based on the horse in Russian steppes
			First highway system built in Assyria
			Homer composes *Iliad* and *Odyssey*
		700	Rome founded
		200	Wheelbarrow invented in China
			Epics about India's gods and heroes, the *Mahabharata* and *Ramayana*, written
			Water wheel invented in Middle East
		0	Christian era begins

▼ Two thousand million years ago

▼ One thousand million years ago

First oxygen-breathing animals (900 million) ▲

First animals to possess ▲
backbones (470 million)

First men (1.3 million) ▲

Credits

The sources for the illustrations in this book are shown below. Credits from left to right are separated by semicolons, from top to bottom by dashes.

Cover—Geoffrey Gove from Photo Trends. 8 —C. M. Dixon. 12—The Tourist Photo Library, London; C. M. Dixon—W. F. Davidson from Bruce Coleman, Inc. 14 to 17—Nicholas Fasciano. 19—Dr. Georg Gerster from Rapho-Guillumette. 21 to 24—Plans from *The Prehistoric Antiquities of the Maltese Islands: A Survey*, by J. D. Evans. The Althone Press, 1971. Plans made possible by a grant from the University of Malta. Photographs by C. M. Dixon. 26, 27 —Scala. 29 to 32—George V. Kelvin. 35 to 41—Daniel Maffia. 42—Eileen Tweedy courtesy Museum of the Wiltshire Archaeological and Natural History Society, Devizes. 45—John R. Freeman courtesy the Society of Antiquaries, London. 48, 49, 50 —Michael A. Hampshire. 52—John R. Freeman courtesy the Society of Antiquaries, London. 55—Photo Bibliothèque Nationale, Paris. 57—Courtesy the New York Public Library. 58—The Master and Fellows of Corpus Christi College, Cambridge; Courtesy the New York Public Library. 59—Courtesy the New York Public Library. 60—John R. Freeman courtesy the Society of Antiquaries, London. 62—Nicholas Fasciano. 64—Museum of the Wiltshire Archaeological and Natural History Society, Devizes. 71—Salisbury and South Wiltshire Museum—Eileen Tweedy courtesy Museum of the Wiltshire Archaeological and Natural History Society, Devizes. 74 to 79—Jack Endewelt. 80 —Eileen Tweedy courtesy Museum of the Wiltshire Archaeological and Natural History Society, Devizes. 84, 85—Eileen Tweedy courtesy Museum of the Wiltshire Archaeological and Natural History Society, Devizes; Salisbury and South Wiltshire Museum. 86—Nicholas Fasciano. 88—Eileen Tweedy courtesy Museum of the Wiltshire Archaeological and Natural History Society, Devizes—Eileen Tweedy courtesy the Trustees of the British Museum. 89—Eileen Tweedy courtesy Museum of the Wiltshire Archaeological and Natural History Society, Devizes; Eileen Tweedy courtesy Museum of the Wiltshire Archaeological and Natural History Society, Devizes—Eileen Tweedy courtesy Dorset County Museum. 91—Eileen Tweedy courtesy Salisbury and South Wiltshire Museum—Eileen Tweedy courtesy Museum of the Wiltshire Archaeological and Natural History Society, Devizes. 92—C. M. Dixon. 94—Eileen Tweedy courtesy the Trustees of the British Museum. 96, 97—C. M. Dixon. 99, 100, 101—The Tourist Photo Library, London. 102, 103—British Crown Copyright: reproduced by the permission of the Department of the Environment. 104 —Georges Devy. 106—C. M. Dixon. 107—C. M. Dixon; Michael A. Hampshire. 110, 111 —Drawings by George V. Kelvin based on drawings from *Megalithic Lunar Observations* by Alexander Thom, © Oxford University Press, 1971. 114—Dr. Georg Gerster from Rapho-Guillumette. 115—George V. Kelvin. 119 to 129—Michael A. Hampshire. 130—The Bodleian Library, Oxford, MS. Gough Maps 231. 134—Roger-Viollet. 137 —Archives Photographiques. 139—Courtesy the New York Public Library. 140, 141—Photo Bibliothèque Nationale, Paris. 145 to 149—J. S. Lewinski. 150, 151—Flip Schulke from Rapho-Guillumette. 152, 153—Bullaty-Lomeo from Rapho-Guillumette.

Quotes on page 73: from the poetry of Hesiod reprinted from Richmond Lattimore's translation of Hesiod, *The Works and Days*, lines 112, 116-119. Copyright © the University of Michigan, 1959. Reprinted by permission of the University of Michigan Press.

Acknowledgments

For the help given in the preparation of this book, the editors are particularly indebted to the following people and institutions: Kenneth Annable, Curator, Devizes Museum, Devizes, England; Professor Richard J. C. Atkinson, Head of the Department of Archaeology, University College, Cardiff, Wales; Gérard Bailloud, Research Assistant, National Center for Scientific Research, Paris; Mauricette Bailloud, Musée Miln-Le Rouzic, Carnac-Ville, France; Seamus Caulfield, Department of Archaeology, University College, Dublin; Dorset County Museum, Dorchester, England; Pierre Roland Giot, Director of Research for the National Center of Scientific Research, Faculty of Sciences, Rennes, France; Peter Harbison, Archaeological Advisor, Department of National Monuments, Irish Tourist Board, Dublin; Michael Herity, Department of Archaeology, University College, Dublin; Professor G. Evelyn Hutchinson, Sterling Professor Emeritus of Zoology, Yale University, New Haven, Connecticut; Maurice Jacq, Honorary Curator, Musée Miln-Le Rouzic, Carnac-Ville, France; Charles Le Roux, Director of Prehistoric Antiquities of Brittany, Faculty of Sciences, Rennes, France; C. A. Newham, Tadcaster, Yorkshire, England; Seán O Nualláin, Archaeology Officer, Ordnance Survey of Ireland, Dublin; Dr. Elizabeth K. Ralph, Associate Director, Museum Applied Science Center for Archaeology (MASCA), University of Pennsylvania; Salisbury and South Wiltshire Museum, Salisbury, England; Society of Antiquaries, London; Dr. Alexander Thom, Emeritus Professor of Engineering Science, Oxford University, England; Jean-Yves Vieillard, Curator of the Musée de Bretagne, Rennes, France.

Bibliography

General

Arribas, Antonio, *The Iberians*. Frederick A. Praeger, 1964.

Butzer, Karl W., *Environment and Archaeology*, Methuen, 1972.

Chadwick, Nora K., *Celtic Britain*, Ancient Peoples and Places Series, Thames and Hudson, 1963.

Childe, V. Gordon, *Man Makes Himself*, Fontana, 1966.

Clark, Grahame, *World Prehistory, An Outline*, Cambridge University Press, 1969.

Clarke, D. L., *Beaker Pottery of Great Britain and Ireland*, Cambridge University Press, 1970.

Coles, John, ed., *Proceedings of the Prehistoric Society; Contributions to Prehistory Offered to Grahame Clarke*. The Prehistoric Society, 1971.

Coles, J. M. and Simpson, D. D. A., eds., *Studies in Ancient Europe*, Leicester University Press, 1968.

Crampton, Patrick, *Stonehenge of the Kings*. John Day, 1968.

Daniel, Glyn E.:
The Hungry Archaeologist in France, Faber, 1963.
The Idea of Prehistory, C. A. Watts, 1962.
Origins and Growth of Archaeology, Penguin Books, 1967.

Davidson, Hilda Roderick Ellis, *Pagan Scandinavia*, Ancient Peoples and Places Series, Thames and Hudson, 1967.

Fox, Cyril, and Bruce Dickins, eds., *The Early Cultures of North-West Europe (H. M. Chadwick Memorial Studies)*. Cambridge University Press, 1950.

Graves, Robert:
The Greek Myths, Cassell, 1958.
The Greek Myths, Penguin Books, 1969.
White Goddess, Faber, 1952.

Hawkes, C. F. C., *The Prehistoric Foundations of Europe*. Methuen & Co. Ltd., 1940.

Heyerdahl, Thor, *Aku-Aku*, Allen and Unwin, 1958.

James, E. O., *The Cult of the Mother-God-*

dess. Thames and Hudson, 1959.

Kendrick, Sir Thomas, *British Antiquity*, Library Reprints, Methuen, 1970.

Kennedy, Charles W., translator, *Beowulf, The Oldest English Epic*. Oxford University Press, 1940.

Kininmonth, Christopher, *Malta and Gozo*, Travellers' Guides, Jonathan Cape, 1970.

Lattimore, Richmond, translator, *Hesiod*. University of Michigan Press, 1968.

Lee, Richard B., and Irven DeVore, *Man the Hunter*. Aldine, 1968.

Lethbridge, T. C., *Gogmagog: The Buried Gods*, Routledge and Kegan Paul, 1957.

Maringer, Johannes, *The Gods of Prehistoric Man*, Weidenfeld and Nicolson, 1960.

Michell, John, *The View Over Atlantis*, Garnstone Press, 1969.

Neustupny, Evzen and Jiri, *Czechoslovakia*. Frederick A. Praeger, 1961.

O'Kelly, Claire, *Guide to New Grange*. John English & Co. Ltd., 1971.

Pfeiffer, John E., *The Emergence of Man*, Thomas Nelson, 1970.

Piggott, Stuart, *Ancient Europe: A Survey*, Edinburgh University Press, 1965.

Piggott, Stuart and Daniel, Glyn, *A Picture Book of Ancient British Art*, Cambridge University Press, 1951.

Powell, Anthony, *John Aubrey and his Friends*, Heinemann, 1963.

Powell, T. G. E., *The Celts*. Thames and Hudson, 1959.

Savory, Hubert Newman, *Spain and Portugal*, Ancient Peoples and Places Series, Thames and Hudson, 1968.

Service, Elman R., *Primitive Social Organization, An Evolutionary Perspective*. Random House, 1971.

Stern, Philip van Doren, *Prehistoric Europe: From Stone Age Man to the Early Greeks*, Allen and Unwin, 1970.

Taylour, Lord William, *The Mycenaeans*, Ancient Peoples and Places Series, Thames and Hudson, 1964.

Tringham, Ruth, *Hunters, Fishers and Farmers of Eastern Europe, 6000-3000 B.C.*, Hutchinson University Library, 1971.

The Megaliths

Atkinson, R. J. C., *Stonehenge*. Hamish Hamilton, 1956.

Daniel, Glyn E.:
The Megalith Builders of Western Europe, Hutchinson University Library, 1963.
The Prehistoric Chamber Tombs of France, Thames and Hudson, 1960.

Evans, J. D., *The Prehistoric Antiquities of the Maltese Islands*, Athlone Press, 1971.

Fox, Alleen, *South West England*, Frederick A. Praeger, 1964.

Giot, Pierre, *Brittany* (in collaboration with J. L'Helgouach and J. Briard). Frederick A. Praeger, 1960.

Glob, P. V., *Danish Prehistoric Monuments; Denmark from the Stone Age to the Vikings*, Faber, 1971.

Hawkins, Gerald S. (in collaboration with John B. White), *Stonehenge Decoded*. Doubleday and Company, Inc., 1965.

Jessup, Ronald, *South East England*, Ancient Peoples and Places Series, Thames and Hudson, 1970.

Jensen, O. Klindt-, *Denmark Before the Vikings*, Ancient Peoples and Places Series, Thames and Hudson, 1957.

O'Riordain, Sean P., and Daniel Glyn, E., *New Grange*, Ancient People and Places Series, Thames and Hudson, 1964.

Piggott, Stuart:
The Neolithic Cultures of the British Isles. Cambridge University Press, 1970.
The West Kennet Long Barrow, Excavations 1955-56. Ministry of Works Archaeological Reports, No. 4, 1962.

Stone, J. F. S., *Wessex*. Frederick A. Praeger, 1960.

Thom, Alexander:
Megalithic Lunar Observatories. Oxford University Press, 1971.
Megalithic Sites in Britain. Oxford University Press, 1967.

Index

Numerals in italics indicate an illustration of the subject mentioned.

Filmsetting by C. E. Dawkins (Typesetters) Ltd., London, SE1 1UN

Printed and bound in Belgium by Brepols Fabrieken N.V.